The Church Ladies'
Divine Desserts

AN ELLEN ROLFES BOOK

G. P. Putnam's Sons

New York

The Church Ladies' Divine Desserts

Heavenly Recipes and Sweet Recollections

Brenda Rhodes Miller

G. P. Putnam's Sons
Publishers Since 1838
a member of
Penguin Putnam Inc.
375 Hudson St.
New York, NY 10014

A list of contributors and cookbooks appears on pages 187–190.

Library of Congress Cataloging-in-Publication Data

Miller, Brenda Rhodes.
The church ladies' divine desserts : heavenly recipes and sweet recollections / Brenda Rhodes Miller.
p.   cm.
Includes index.
ISBN 0-399-14780-2
1. Desserts.   I. Title.
TX773.M533   2001   2001018593
641.8'6—dc21

Printed in the United States of America
1   3   5   7   9   10   8   6   4   2

This book is printed on acid-free paper. ∞

BOOK DESIGN BY AMANDA DEWEY

ACKNOWLEDGMENTS

Thank you" is such a teeny-tiny, insufficient, little bit of a phrase. It hardly begins to convey the enormous debt of gratitude I feel for all the people, living and dead, who brought this book to life. Rather than struggle to find creative ways to say "Thank you," I will simply express my sincere appreciation to each one and beg forgiveness of anyone I may have overlooked. I am grateful to them all.

Thank you to Mrs. Beulah Hughes for her lesson of keeping promises; to my Aunt Dot and Sister Consilio for sharing their wisdom; to Philonese Thompson, Mrs. Ross, Mrs. Bertha Woods, Mrs. Seals, Carol Preston, and Mrs. McCreary for being ideal church ladies in every way; to my dear parents, Charles and Lolita Rhodes, for bringing me up with love in the church; to my grandmother Lottie Twyner Rhodes for teaching me to be generous; to my Aunt Julie and my Aunt Bessie Ruth, who told me the old family stories; to my Aunt Doris for her sense of humor; to my Uncle Wiley and Aunt Willie Creagh, who gave me the courage to tackle this marvelous subject; to my blood sisters Nanny Med and Nanny Letie for their Christian example, their funny stories, and their suggestions; to Cousin Joyce Ladner and my "pretend" sisters, Beverly Easton, Dora

Finley, Sharon Robinson, Joyce Felder, Edy Crump, and Fourthy, for encouraging me to keep writing; to my sister-under-the-skin, Ellen Rolfes, for her firm belief in the transforming power of the meal table; to my mentor, Dr. Height, for her inspiration and support; to Judith T. Kern, who gently overcame my fear of editors; to Carol Boker for having each recipe faithfully tested; to my patient children, Lauren, Jay, and Ben Cooper, who gave me the time to write; to Lita, who kept the home fires burning while I was otherwise engaged; to my capital "A" agent, Liv Blumer, who laughed with me about our mutual search for big-head hats, and who loved the idea of a church lady cookbook; to publisher John Duff, whose fondness for fruitcake remains a mystery to me and who brought the project to the public.

Special thanks and blessings to my husband, Rev. Courtenay Miller, who had to read every word I wrote at least five times, and my father-in-law, Rev. Clarence Miller, without whose help I would never have been able to write this book.

In my home church, Mrs. Early L. Rush introduces herself to visitors by saying, "I'm always Early, never Late, always in a Rush." Thanks to her and every other church lady who shared herself with me through a story, a recipe, or a photograph for this book.

Mrs. Early L. Rush, left, and Mrs. Bertha Woods welcome a new generation student to Sunday School.

CONTENTS

FOREWORD

As a child, I lived right next door to Emmanuel Baptist Church in Rankin, Pennsylvania. I grew up helping out in the church kitchen, where Mrs. Mary Reynolds ran the Hospitality Committee with skill, grace, and an iron hand. It was there, under Mrs. Reynolds's tutelage, that I learned to volunteer.

A tall, striking woman with dark brown skin, Mrs. Reynolds contained her abundant salt-and-pepper gray hair under an invisible net while working in the kitchen. Since the Hospitality Committee did much of its work before and after services, we were all instructed to wear immaculate aprons over our clothes, as protection against spills. Mrs. Reynolds set equally strict standards for the food served at church events. Her cardinal rule was that any food donated by church members must be fresh, homemade, and delicious. Unfortunately, when the food failed to meet her exacting culinary expectations, she did not bite her tongue. Mrs. Reynolds had a lot to say to members who brought food that failed to pass muster.

I can see her now, hands planted on her abundant hips as she called for a pan of hot rolls, only to be confronted with a loaf of cold, dry, store-bought bread. The exasperation in her voice when she announced "We don't serve light bread here" was surpassed only by her dismay when she discovered a member had brought in a cake that clearly was not made from scratch. With a sniff, her emphatic "We don't serve box cakes here" dismissed the offending dessert from her sight.

Reading the stories of churchwomen written by my friend Brenda Rhodes Miller in *The Church Ladies' Divine Desserts* reminds me of Mrs. Reynolds. Midway through arranging for a big church event—and big events always called for food—Mrs. Reynolds would turn her eyes heavenward and say, "Jesus, if I can just make it in!" Like Mrs. Reynolds, the women profiled here have struggled and endured, leaning on their faith for strength "to make it in." Their efforts have built and maintained African-American culture by supporting one of our most central institutions after the family, that institution being the church.

It has long been said, "Black women may not always do what we want, but we always do what we must." Nowhere is this more apparent than in church. When I was a child, it was taken as an article of faith at Emmanuel Baptist Church that while men might rule the church, certainly women ran it. Today, many women have risen to highly visible leadership positions such as pastors and preachers, roles formerly occupied only by men. But all over America, many other women still work behind the scenes in relative obscurity, devoting their time, their energy, and their financial contributions to making sure the church runs as it should.

Dr. Dorothy I. Height

In many congregations, women far outnumber men. As a result, there are few tasks to which churchwomen have not lent a hand, from landscape beautification projects to mortgage-burning ceremonies. Churchwomen are renowned for their tireless organizing efforts and their hard work. Would there ever be a building drive, stewardship campaign, vacation Bible school, foreign mission, voter registration project, health fair, or Christian adult literacy initiative in this country without the efforts of these women? In addition, women continue to be the backbone of traditional church work, providing help to the sick and shut-in, managing choirs and music ministries, teaching Sunday schools, serving on usher boards, and organizing fund-raisers.

Each summer, the National Council of Negro Women invites people from all over the country to join in the Black Family Reunion. This national celebration honors the strength and resiliency of African-American families throughout the history of this country. There, as at church gatherings throughout America, people sit together and talk with one another over food. Since 1986, the Black Family Reunion has been a time to pass along family stories and to share treasured recipes and photographs with loved ones. Enjoying an old-fashioned meal finished off with a familiar and lovingly prepared dessert is an experience that connects strangers and builds bonds of friendship at the Black Family Reunion and everywhere.

In tribute to Mrs. Mary McLeod Bethune, founder of the National Council of Negro Women, and herself a devoted and well-known churchwoman, we have included her recipe for sweet potato pie in this book. I encourage you to make it for someone you love. *The Church Ladies' Divine Desserts* celebrates the role churchwomen have played in preserving our culture by preparing desserts and maintaining the traditions that unite us. As I read their stories, tears came to my eyes. Frequently, they were tears of laughter as I recognized the often insightful, sometimes acerbic, but always trenchant sayings and expressions of these memorable women. Other times, my tears were a homage to the valiant women like Mrs. Mary Reynolds and Mrs. Mary McLeod Bethune, who relied on faith and hard work to "make it in."

The pleasures of eating the desserts in *The Church Ladies' Divine Desserts* may be ephemeral, but the wise lessons of these and all churchwomen endure.

Dorothy Irene Height

INTRODUCTION

What determines who is a church lady and who is not? Regular attendance at Sunday worship alone does not a church lady make. Nor does any other single factor have the power to elevate an ordinary woman to the ranks of church ladyship. True church ladies are women of many parts. They hold together African-American culture with their prayers, good works, life lessons, wit, talent, humor, determination, organizational abilities, resilience, and abundant love. The true church ladies of this world indeed attend worship religiously. They give their money in tithes and offerings, they give their time in service, and they live their faith on a daily basis.

As I interviewed African-American women from churches all over the country for this book, I was humbled both by their dedicated service and by their abiding faith. I heard stories from Christian women who are ushers, singers, stewards, mothers of the church, missionaries, youth workers, clerks, fund-raisers, members of hospitality committees, first ladies, Sunday school teachers, tithers, faithful pew members, and musicians. I listened to women talk about their work as historians, librarians, photographers, financial planners, gardeners, actors, orators, and community development experts. Each served God by using her considerable skills to serve her church. Perhaps best of all were the stories about church ladies who had inspired others to follow in their footsteps.

Vigilant guardians of our culture, church ladies continue to mold and shape new generations by their insistence on the primacy of the family meal table. In many homes, a kitchen or dining room table does double and triple duty. The family meal table is where important discussions take place, where the elders gather over cake and coffee to make decisions and plans. Children often do their lessons at this table, with a few cookies and a glass of milk to tide them over until their supper. The evening meal made by a mother, an aunt, an older sister, or a grandmother who keeps the children company while she cooks is the best meal of the day. And, of course, the table is where families gather to share food and conversation. Blessed when grace is said, even the hastiest meal becomes a special event if there is a dessert, no matter how simple it may be.

Busy people, grieving people, suffering people, tired people who confront sour discrimination and the bitterness of injustice welcome the comfort of a familiar dessert made with love. A homemade dessert is more than just a sweet finale to a meal. In the African-American kitchen, desserts provide a way to show off one's culinary skill and to demonstrate special affection while underscoring the bounty of God's blessings on the home. Desserts are an indulgence.

A church lady puts the final touches on her labor of love—cleaning up before Sunday service. Solomon's Island, MD.

It is one thing to prepare a sturdy, nutritious family meal. It is quite another to use one's precious time and ingredients to crown that meal with a delicious homemade dessert. Unlike the meal itself, dessert is not essential. One could probably live an entire lifetime and never eat dessert, but what a dreary life that would be!

If living well is the best revenge, surely making dessert is one tangible way of thumbing one's nose at too little time, too little money, too little respect, too little everything. Church meals, like family meals, are times for fellowship and the enjoyment that comes with being part of a community. Others may content themselves with fruit and cheese, but no self-respecting African-American church meal is ever complete without a "real" dessert. Trying to pass off simple sweet summer berries as dessert fools no one, though berries are a healthy alternative to rich desserts. But when those berries are piled high on homemade shortcake and smothered with sweetened whipped cream, it's another story entirely.

Desserts that take some doing, such as banana pudding topped with golden meringue, cheesecake covered with blueberry compote, and pound cake with a crumb fine as face powder will satisfy any sweet tooth.

Church ladies understand this and keep the dessert table covered with their homemade treats. When a true church lady goes on to Glory, she is mourned by young and old alike. Their personal loss is often compounded by the loss of the recipe for her special dessert. No one will ever make it the way she did, and without a recipe, no one even knows where to start. In my family, we continue to lament our folly in not writing down Aunt Zefferine's buttermilk sherbet recipe or Grandmother's recipe for sweet potato munge. There is always someone to speak the name of the dear departed church lady in loving memory. But more to the point, there is always someone to say "I would give my soul for a slice of Miss Nelly Anne's lemon ice box pie, the one she always brought to the church picnic!" and mean it.

Church ladies, especially members of hospitality committees, Helping Hands Groups, Wee Willing Workers, Good Samaritan Clubs, Culinary Ministries, or other groups charged with preparing food, are unfailingly frugal with the church's resources. They hold the saying "Waste not, want not" as an article of faith. It was probably a church lady who first announced, "save your fork!" Her intention may have been to collect all the plastic forks, to wash and sterilize them for use at another meal. Or, it may have been to remind everyone that the best was yet to come and dessert was on its way and a fork would be needed to enjoy the cobblers, pies, and cakes that were to come.

Whatever the case, this book is a tribute to church ladies. They always see what needs to be done and do it, usually without being asked, always without expecting to be thanked. Church ladies are something special and apart.

In addition to their service to the church, one thing that sets them apart is each woman's intense devotion to her own particular congregation. They may not always agree with their pastor and they may not always like the ways things are done. But nine times out of ten, they stay put and they stay involved. Church ladies don't just sit back and snipe at the way things are going, though they rarely suffer in silence, either. Most of the time, they get in the thick of it, roll up their sleeves, and put things to right. Or they die trying. Church ladies are rarely "church hoppers," moving from church to church seeking one to meet their needs. Instead, they stay where they are, offering what they know, what they have, and what they are, to making their own church flourish.

I heard the story of one longtime church member who was appalled by the arrival of a new "jit-terbug" pastor. He introduced drums and guitars and a modern, free-flowing style of worship into an old, established congregation that prided itself on its traditions and its orderly services. While she loathed the changes the pastor was making, she continued to attend church and to do the work she had done all her life. She also opened an escrow account for her tithes, holding them there while she agitated for his transfer!

Regardless of denomination, church ladies are the movers and shakers in the congregation. When a church needs someone to organize, chaperone, pray all night, polish the brass, attend a conference or a convention, wash windows, or spearhead a fund-raising campaign, it is the church ladies who step up to the plate. Church ladies can always be counted on to decorate for holidays, prepare food for funerals, reach out to the unchurched, design a new bulletin, construct banners, sew costumes, and clean the chandeliers and bathrooms if that's what needs to be done.

But perhaps even more important than their actual work is the influence church ladies exer-cise. They pass on the standards of their church, teaching children how to behave at worship, demonstrating the value of strong marriages and good parenting. In short, church ladies lead by example. This "invisible" leadership is the secret of the church lady's power. It isn't all sunshine and roses for African-American church ladies. They chafe at being stereotyped as cold, unfeeling, humorless sticks. Worse yet are the media images of them as loud and rambunctious, garishly dressed caricatures wearing large, ridiculous hats, behaving like wild women, and fainting all over the place.

True enough, there are hats aplenty in black churches. On the Saturday before Easter, I vis-ited my neighborhood milliner, looking for a big-head hat to wear on Easter Sunday. (I wore one of the largest graduation caps in my high school class, and finding a hat to fit me is always a chal-lenge.) At five o'clock in the evening, there were church ladies double-parked outside the shop. They were there either to pick up their custom-made chapeaux or to select an off-the-rack hat and get it sized and decorated for one of the major hat-wearing days in the Christian calendar.

Like much of church life, this hat thing is part of the culture. For African-American women of a certain age, being a lady at all times and in all places is mandatory, and nowhere more so than in church, where they continue the tradition by teaching young girls how to be ladies, too. Being a church lady back in the day meant presenting a certain image, always hatted and gloved, per-haps stylish, certainly appropriate.

What mattered most was being a lady. Holding one's head high, sitting with one's back straight, and never raising one's voice were some of the lessons church ladies taught little girls along with the Ten Commandments and the Beatitudes. Church ladies used the resources at hand, in this case worship services and congregational life, to teach generations of Black children that they

Church ladies at Warren Street United Methodist Church put on serious faces for the camera sometime after World War II.

must behave in a certain way if they wished to be accepted by polite society. For church ladies were, most of all, teachers.

In the bad old days, there weren't a lot of opportunities for African-American church ladies to dress up, look sharp, and be treated with respect. Church was one place where they could exercise leadership, be someone special, and mark that distinction with fancy clothes. During segregation, where else could a woman who spent her days dealing with people who refused to acknowledge her humanity be accorded such dignity and respect? Where else could Sally be called Mrs. Anderson? Where else could a talented woman use her gifts? Where else could she thrive? Only in her church.

If you were a child who grew up with church ladies, this book is for you. Now and again, may your head be filled with the scent of rose-water-and-glycerin hand lotion, a whiff of lavender cologne, the smell of freshly boiled starch, or the aroma of apple crumb cake rich with cinnamon. May these dear and familiar fragrances awaken in you the memory of a wonderful woman who made you what you are and the church what it is. Try to remember the pride you felt when a church lady deposited her big, shiny, black patent-leather pocketbook on your lap for safekeeping while she stepped forward to make an announcement. Never forget that there was always a church lady ready to pass starlight mints to quiet fretful children. Those red-and-white candies in their noisy cellophane wrappers were a bribe that seldom failed. If it did, and the misbehavior continued, the church lady's warm brown eyes would become hard as rust. Remember?

I talked to scores of church ladies during the writing of this book. As women will, they welcomed me into their circle of friendship by telling me stories about their lives. From two elderly sisters I learned a foolproof way to get through menopause. Though not twins, they always dress alike and do everything together, including singing in the choir and preparing food for their church's monthly Family and Friends meal. They credit finding happy things to do as a remedy more effective than hormone replacement for successfully navigating the change of life.

The church ladies I met were as varied and interesting as the African-American community itself. Some could see humor everywhere, telling me preacher jokes and poking fun at themselves and their lives. Others were more serious, admonishing me to be sure I understood not only what they said, but also what they meant.

I'm a veteran of sixteen years of Catholic school education, and I grew up in the United Methodist Church, where I taught Sunday school for ten years. My childhood was spent helping my AME Zion grandmother, who was a communion steward, and I recently married a Baptist preacher. Even with all that preparation, discovering church ladies for this book introduced me to new worlds. I hope it does the same for you.

CHAPTER 1

Cakes

Church of God and Saints of Christ members.

I Stand at the Door and Knock

Ushers in the Black church could teach United Nations peacekeepers a thing or two. Renowned for their ability to maintain order in the face of competing priorities, church ushers, as the saying goes, "Know how to handle their business." Without uttering a single word, they guard entry to the sanctuary, seat late congregants, identify empty pews, quiet restless children, carry out instructions from the pulpit, soothe fussy babies, hand out envelopes for the offering, make change for large bills, provide tissues to weeping members, and pass the collection plates. And all this is accomplished through an elaborate system of silent, white-gloved hand signals and ritualized movements. In this secret language, for example, a closed hand held at the base of the throat is the sign for "Attention!" A hand held straight down at the side signifies "I understand." Only in baseball are there more complicated hand signs.

In many churches, there are more usher boards than you can shake a stick at, each one drawing its members based on age and gender. The Junior Usher Board includes teenagers who have graduated from the ranks of the Youth Usher Board, where the youngest members serve. Adults, depending on their age, may be in the Young Adults Usher Board or the Senior Usher Board,

Usher badge.

which is further subdivided into Men's and Ladies' groups. Large churches divide their Senior Usher Boards even further, into Usher Boards Numbers One, Two, Three, and so on, until either all the numbers are used up or they run out of members. This numbering of usher boards can get tricky. The boards might be awarded their numbers or ranking from the order in which they were established, Usher Board Number One being the first and Usher Board Number Three the most recent. Or, they might get their numbers based on how important they are to the life of the church. Sometimes, there are so many members wanting to serve as ushers, and so many services, that multiple boards of senior ushers are required.

Many churches hold early-morning worship, the usual eleven-o'clock service, a Sunday evening service, and a midweek service, as well as special programs throughout the month. Every service needs ushers to keep things running smoothly.

Each usher board has its own uniform, ranging from simple to elaborate, with seasonal color variations based on the weather. Only the ever-present white gloves remain unchanged, no matter the season.

In winter, members of the Ladies' Usher Board typically will wear somber colors like black or navy blue, accented with crisp white blouses. Some wear bow ties; others wear scarves in the colors of the church. A fairly recent innovation is the kente cloth stole, usually seen on ushers with an Afrocentric bent. In summer, ushers perform their duties dressed in white, distinguished from the church nurses only by the absence of the nurse's little white cap. But, regardless of their uniform or when they serve, most ushers wear a badge that announces their function. For ladies, this badge can be a fancy, ruffled handkerchief centered with a shining name tag, or a plain, wide ribbon bearing the name of the church, the title "Usher," and a band of fringe on the bottom. Even without the badge, however, the silent authority of church ushers lets everyone know who they are.

Angel Food Cake

Wonderful all by itself, angel food cake is the perfect "plain" cake, as sweet and light as a child's whispered prayer. Angel food cake is delicious with a fresh fruit topping or a bit of whipped cream.

MAKES 10 TO 12 SERVINGS

1 cup sifted cake flour
1 cup egg whites (8–9 large eggs)
Pinch of salt
1 teaspoon cream of tartar
1¼ cups sugar
¾ teaspoon vanilla extract
¼ teaspoon almond or coconut extract

• • • Preheat the oven to 325°F. Sift the flour three times; set aside. Beat the egg whites and salt. When foamy, add the cream of tartar and continue beating until eggs are stiff but not dry. Fold in the sugar carefully, a small amount at a time. Fold in the vanilla and almond extracts. Fold in the flour, sifting a small amount at a time over mixture. Bake in an ungreased 10-inch tube pan for about 1 hour. Remove pan from oven and invert for 1 hour over a plate before removing cake from the pan.

—Ms. Dora Finley

Spicy Devil's Food Cake

Who knows what misguided soul first decided to slander chocolate cake with the label "devil's food"? This recipe, which combines chocolate and spices in the most heavenly way, might be just the one to set the record straight.

MAKES 12 SERVINGS

1 cup butter
2 cups packed light brown sugar
2 large eggs, well beaten
1 cup buttermilk
4 squares baking chocolate, melted
3 cups all-purpose flour
1½ tablespoons cinnamon
1 teaspoon allspice
1 teaspoon ground cloves
1 teaspoon baking soda
½ cup boiling water
1 teaspoon vanilla
Caramel Frosting (page 184)

• • • Preheat the oven to 350°F. Cream the butter and the sugar in a large bowl. Add the eggs. Stir in the buttermilk and chocolate. Combine the flour, cinnamon, allspice, and cloves in a large bowl; add to the creamed mixture. Dissolve the baking soda in the boiling water. Add to the creamed mixture. Stir in the vanilla. Pour the batter into two greased 9-inch round baking pans. Bake for 30 minutes.

Remove from the oven and cool on wire racks. Remove the cake from the pans and frost with Caramel Frosting.

—Ms. Dora Finley

. . . .

German Sweet Chocolate Cake

Every church lady worth her salt guards her own treasured recipe for this old-fashioned favorite. It has become a holiday tradition in many families.

MAKES 12 TO 14 SERVINGS

4 ounces Baker's sweet chocolate
½ cup water
1 cup butter or margarine
2 cups sugar
4 large eggs, separated
1 teaspoon vanilla
2½ cups sifted cake flour
1 teaspoon baking soda
½ teaspoon salt
1 cup buttermilk
Frosting

• • • Preheat the oven to 350°F. Line the bottoms of 3 (9-inch) round cake pans with waxed paper. Melt the chocolate in the ½ cup of water in the top of a double boiler; cool. Cream the butter and sugar in a large bowl until fluffy. Add the egg yolks, one at a time, beating well after each addition. Blend in the

vanilla and chocolate. Sift the flour with the baking soda and salt in a medium bowl. Add alternately with the buttermilk to the chocolate mixture, beating after each addition until smooth. Beat the egg whites in a medium bowl until stiff peaks form. Fold into the batter. Pour into the prepared pans. Bake 30 to 40 minutes or until done; cool. Add the frosting between the layers and over the top and sides.

FROSTING

1 (12-ounce) can evaporated milk
1½ cups sugar
¾ cup butter or margarine
4 large egg yolks, slightly beaten
1½ teaspoons vanilla
1 (7-ounce) package flaked coconut
1½ cups chopped pecans

Mix the milk, sugar, butter, egg yolks, and vanilla in a medium saucepan. Cook, stirring constantly, over medium heat about 12 minutes or until thickened and golden brown. Remove from the heat. Stir in the coconut and pecans. Cool to room temperature before spreading.

—Mrs. La Ruth Pryor

. . . .

If I Can Talk, I Can Pray. If I Can Walk, I Can Go to Church

MRS. BEULAH HUGHES

Toulminville-Warren UMC

Mobile, Alabama

Fifty-two Sundays a year for fifty years. Can you imagine that? Mrs. Beulah Hughes, who celebrated her one hundredth birthday August 5, 2000, was a Sunday school teacher for fifty years until her recent retirement.

The wife of a preacher, Mrs. Hughes did not attend her husband's church. She had her own place in her own church, where she was a faithful member—reliable, steadfast, and quiet in her service. "Salt of the earth" is a phrase often used to describe her and, in every way, Beulah Hughes has been a model Christian who gave her all until she was "all give out."

The word *humble* has fallen out of favor in this age so much concerned with self-esteem. But Mrs. Hughes is humble in the most Christian sense of the word. She never looks for or expects any thanks and is frankly embarrassed when notice is taken of what she considers her duty.

Mrs. Hughes is also a fabulous cook. Even when she had to lean on a cane to stand, she was still making cakes—airy confections so light they almost floated into your mouth. She isn't stingy with her recipes, either, and shares them willingly with anyone who asks; though no one can ever quite duplicate her astonishing results. Perhaps that's because Mrs. Hughes added some special, secret ingredients to her fruitcake cookies, her cheese straws, and caramel pound cake. Those secret ingredients were her endless love and affection, her boundless joy, and her devotion to God.

Mrs. Beulah Hughes, who taught Sunday School for fifty years, rests from her labors as she sits on her front porch.

Buttermilk Chocolate Cake

Pity the poor children—anyone, for that matter—who turn up their noses at the thought of buttermilk. They are sure to miss the pleasure of a special dessert often served at church suppers.

MAKES 14 TO 16 SERVINGS

2 cups all-purpose flour

2 cups sugar

2 sticks butter or margarine

4 tablespoons unsweetened cocoa powder

1 cup water

½ cup buttermilk

1 teaspoon vanilla

1 teaspoon cinnamon

¼ teaspoon salt

1 teaspoon baking soda

2 large eggs

Frosting

• • •Preheat the oven to 400°F. Combine flour and sugar in a large bowl. Heat the butter, cocoa, and water in a medium saucepan; bring to a boil. Pour over the dry ingredients and mix well. Add the remaining ingredients; mix. Pour into a greased and floured 13-by-9-inch baking pan. Bake 20 minutes.

Remove from the oven and pour the warm frosting over the top. Cool to allow frosting to set before serving. Serve with vanilla ice cream, if desired.

FROSTING

1 stick butter or margarine

4 tablespoons unsweetened cocoa powder

5 tablespoons milk

1 teaspoon vanilla

1 cup chopped pecans

1 (16-ounce) box powdered sugar

¼ teaspoon cinnamon

Before the cake is done, combine the butter, cocoa, and milk in a saucepan. Heat until butter is melted. Remove from heat; add remaining ingredients. Beat until all ingredients are mixed well. Keep warm.

—Ms. Joyce Felder

Chocolate Mayonnaise Cake

Mayonnaise is more than simply the favored condiment for Vacation Bible School bologna sandwiches. It also adds special moistness and richness to chocolate cake.

MAKES 16 TO 18 SERVINGS

2 cups all-purpose flour

1 teaspoon baking soda

4 tablespoons unsweetened cocoa powder

1½ cups sugar

1 cup mayonnaise

1 cup hot water

1 teaspoon vanilla

• • • Preheat the oven to 350°F. Sift the dry ingredients together in a large bowl. Combine the mayonnaise and hot water in a medium bowl; add the vanilla. Add the mayonnaise mixture to the dry ingredients; mix well. Pour into a greased and floured 13-by-9-inch pan. Bake for 45 to 60 minutes, or until a toothpick inserted in center of cake comes out clean. Add frosting of your choice or serve with ice cream and chocolate sauce.

—*Mrs. Doretha G. Manuel*

Mrs. Flora Moore stands outside Mt. Airy Baptist Church where she is Church Secretary. Her cheerful voice and welcoming demeanor are a treasured part of Mt. Airy, located just blocks from the Capitol. The church is adorned with a sign that proclaims it is "A Monument to Jesus."

Raisin Bundt Cake

No "Hanging of the Greens" pre-Christmas holiday celebration would be complete without this cake. It may remind you of fruitcake, only not as busy and maybe a little bit better.

MAKES 18 TO 20 SERVINGS

½ cup plus 1 teaspoon butter or margarine
1¼ cups sugar
3 large eggs, separated
3¼ cups cake flour
1 teaspoon baking powder
½ cup raisins
2 teaspoons grated lemon rind
¾ cup plus 1½ tablespoons milk
Lemon Glaze (page 185)

• • • Preheat the oven to 375°F. Cream the butter and sugar in a large bowl. Gradually add the egg yolks; beat well. Sift the flour and baking powder in a large bowl; add the raisins and lemon rind to the flour. Add the milk and flour mixture alternately to the butter mixture. Beat the egg whites in a medium bowl until soft peaks form. Fold into the batter. Pour into a greased and floured Bundt pan. Bake for 30 to 40 minutes, or until cake tests done. Turn out onto cake rack after cooling for about 8 minutes. Cool for 10 minutes more. Place cake on a plate. Pierce several times with a skewer. Top with warm Lemon Glaze.

—*Mrs. Flora Moore*

. . . .

Applesauce Cake

After a long Official Board meeting, nothing soothes frazzled spirits like a slice of this homey and delicious little cake accompanied with a nice warm cup of hot tea.

MAKES 9 SERVINGS

1¾ cups sifted cake flour
1 teaspoon baking powder
¼ teaspoon salt
1 teaspoon cinnamon
½ teaspoon nutmeg
1 cup raisins
½ cup shortening
1 cup sugar
1 teaspoon baking soda
1 cup warm applesauce
Orange Frosting (page 179)

• • • Preheat the oven to 350°F. Sift together the flour, baking powder, salt, and spices in a large bowl. Add the raisins. Cream the shortening in a large bowl; slowly add the sugar and cream until fluffy. Stir the baking soda into the warm applesauce in a small bowl. Stir in the

dry ingredients alternately with the warm applesauce; mix well. Spoon the batter into a greased 8-inch square pan. Bake for about 45 minutes or until the cake tests done. Cool and frost with Orange Frosting.

—*Mrs. Bessie Samples*

. . . .

Coconut Layer Cake with Pineapple Filling

An unmistakable herald of spring, Coconut Layer Cake with Pineapple Filling is a star attraction at Good Friday bake sales. Although this cake has many steps, it is well worth the effort . . . especially when someone makes it for you!

MAKES 16 TO 18 SERVINGS

2¼ cups sifted cake flour
1½ cups sugar
3 teaspoons baking powder
1 teaspoon salt
⅔ cup soft shortening
1 cup milk
1½ teaspoons coconut extract
3 large eggs
Pineapple Filling
Pineapple Frosting
¾ cup shredded coconut

• • • Preheat the oven to 350°F. Grease and flour two 9-inch round baking pans. Sift together the flour, sugar, baking powder, and salt in a large bowl. Add the shortening, mixing well. Add half of the milk and the coconut extract; mix well for 2 minutes. Add the remaining milk and the eggs; mix well for 2 minutes. Pour even amounts of batter into the prepared pans, and bake 30 to 35 minutes or until the cake tests done when a wooden pick is inserted. Remove from the oven and cool on wire racks 10 minutes. Turn out on wire racks to cool completely. Place one layer on a serving plate. Cover with Pineapple Filling. Top with second layer of cake. Spread Pineapple Frosting over tops and sides. Cover the top and sides of the frosting with the coconut. Store in the refrigerator.

PINEAPPLE FILLING

½ cup sugar

3 tablespoons cornstarch

½ teaspoon salt

¾ cup pineapple juice

¾–1 cup crushed pineapple, well drained

1 tablespoon butter

1 teaspoon lemon juice

Combine all the ingredients in a medium saucepan; boil for 1 minute, stirring constantly. Chill before using.

PINEAPPLE FROSTING

1 cup sugar

⅓ cup pineapple juice

⅓ teaspoon cream of tartar

2 large egg whites

1½ teaspoons vanilla

Combine the sugar, pineapple juice, and cream of tartar in a small saucepan. Boil slowly, without stirring, until the syrup spins a 6- to 8-inch thread (242°F). Remove from the heat. Keep the pan covered for the first 3 minutes to prevent the crystals from forming on the sides of the pan. Beat the egg whites in a medium bowl until stiff enough to hold a peak. Pour the hot syrup slowly into the egg whites, beating constantly. Add the vanilla. Beat until the frosting holds its shape.

—*Mrs. Carolyn L. Rhodes*

Creamy Lemon Cheesecake

Long before there were restaurants devoted to mass-produced cheesecake, this sophisticated dessert was prepared by West Coast church ladies using lemons from trees in their own backyards.

MAKES 6 TO 8 SERVINGS

CRUST

1 cup graham cracker crumbs

¼ cup sugar

3 tablespoons shortening

FILLING

3 ounces cream cheese

2 cups low-fat (1%) cottage cheese

2 large egg whites

MRS. ELIZA SIMMONS
Warren Street Methodist Church
Mobile, Alabama

E very organization, be it sacred or secular, needs a watchdog group to keep it honest. As long as someone pays attention to the details and is willing to speak up, the mission and integrity of the organization will be safe. According to Dr. Wiley L. Bolden, now of Atlanta, Georgia, when he was a little boy attending the Warren Street Methodist Church, Mrs. Eliza Simmons was the self-appointed, one-woman watchdog group. Dr. Bolden recalls that Mrs. Simmons was relentless in her exercise of due diligence.

When the financial report was read, Mrs. Simmons was all ears. If the report stated she had given $2.50, and that was not the exact amount of her gift, she would raise her hand and politely correct the record to show she had actually given $2.53.

She kept them all on their toes.

½ cup sugar

1 teaspoon freshly grated lemon peel

3 tablespoons fresh lemon juice

1 teaspoon vanilla

● ● ● Preheat the oven to 350°F. For the crust, combine graham cracker crumbs, sugar, and shortening in a bowl. Mix well with fork. Press into the bottom and halfway up the the sides of a 9-inch pie plate.

For the filling, blend the cream cheese and cottage cheese in a food processor or blender until completely smooth. Add egg whites, sugar, lemon peel, juice, and vanilla. Blend well. Pour mixture into crust.

Bake for 30 minutes. Turn oven off and allow cheesecake to remain in oven for 5 minutes. Cool. Refrigerate until cold. Cut into wedges. Garnish with lemon slices or other fresh fruit, if desired.

—*Julia Hardeman-Tsadick*

Orange Cheesecake

Nearly everyone will like this cool and refreshing cheesecake. It combines the flavor of a favorite fruit—the orange—with the mellow richness of cheesecake. Imagine serving it garnished with thin slices of candied orange peel for a bridal shower.

MAKES 12 SERVINGS

1½ cups graham cracker crumbs

3 tablespoons unsweetened cocoa powder

3 tablespoons sugar

4 tablespoons vegetable oil

1 (24-ounce) container cottage cheese

1½ (8-ounce) packages cream cheese

1½ cups sugar

½ cup orange juice concentrate

⅓ cup dry milk powder

2 large eggs

3 large egg whites

2 teaspoons vanilla

¼ teaspoon salt

• • •Preheat the oven to 300°F. Grease a 9-inch springform pan. Combine graham cracker crumbs, cocoa powder, and 3 tablespoons sugar in a medium bowl. Stir in the oil. Press the mixture into the bottom of the prepared pan. Puree the cottage cheese and cream cheese in a blender until smooth. In large bowl, mix the puree, 1½ cups sugar, orange juice concentrate, milk powder, eggs, egg whites, vanilla, and salt. Pour slowly and carefully over the crust in the pan so the mixture does not disturb the crumbs. Bake 1 hour and 15 minutes (center will still be soft).

If desired, decorate with piped whipped cream flavored with lime juice and vanilla. Top with candied orange or lime twists before serving.

—Mrs. Beulah Hughes

Baby Cheesecakes

Add a note of elegance to your church tea by using a footed crystal cake plate to set out individual servings like these Baby Cheesecakes. You can be sure someone will beg for the recipe every time!

MAKES 1½ DOZEN

1 (12-ounce) box vanilla wafers

3 (8-ounce) packages cream cheese

1 cup sugar

3 large eggs

¼ teaspoon nutmeg

1 teaspoon vanilla

• • •Preheat the oven to 325°F. Place 1 vanilla wafer in the bottom of 18 muffin papers in muffin pans. Combine the cream cheese, sugar, eggs, nutmeg, and vanilla in a medium bowl; mix well. Pour on top of vanilla wafers. Bake for 20 to 25 minutes or until a knife inserted in the middle comes out clean. Cool and chill until ready to serve.

—Ms. Julia Hardeman Tsadick

Jelly Roll

This dessert was the specialty of a cloistered nun who made it each year when her family came to visit, but you don't have to live a celibate life to enjoy its goodness.

MAKES 8 TO 10 SERVINGS

3 large eggs
1 cup sugar
3 tablespoons cold water
1 cup all-purpose flour
1 teaspoon baking powder
⅓ teaspoon salt
Powdered sugar
1–1½ cups jam or jelly of your choice

• • • Preheat the oven to 375°F. Beat the eggs and sugar until thick; add the water, then the flour, baking powder, and salt, sifted together twice. Line a 15-by-10-inch jelly roll or shallow pan with greased waxed or parchment paper; pour in the batter evenly, and bake about 12 minutes. Turn out onto a cloth or paper sprinkled with powdered sugar; tear off the paper and spread with jam or jelly. Beginning with the narrow end, roll up quickly. Cool. Slice and dust with additional powdered sugar before serving.

—Mrs. Philonese Thompson

Jelly Roll in the Convent

Cloistered nuns are neither in the world nor of the world. They live silent lives of prayer and contemplation, nurturing loved ones from afar through constant and fervent prayer. Having given up worldly distractions, they rarely see their families. The infrequent visits they are allowed tend to be joyous, albeit brief.

A friend tells the story of visiting an elderly relative who lived in a secluded hillside convent. Goats wandered about within the walls, munching grass and providing milk for the cheese the convent sold to support itself.

Once a year, entire families trooped to the convent—babies, toddlers, teens, and adults of all ages crammed into a tiny, old-fashioned sitting room. A heavy, wrought-iron gate separated the nuns from their visitors in the parlor. Children could stretch their small hands through the metal for a touch of the nuns' holy hands, but adult hands were too large. They could barely do more than brush fingertips, the only physical contact allowed with their beloved relatives.

Each year, in honor of the family visit, the convent served cakes made by the nuns' own hands. Several were highly skilled bakers who supplemented the meager income of the convent by making baked goods that were sold to specialty stores. One of their most popular items was a jelly roll, and my friend, a callous teenager at the time, found it hilarious that professional virgins baked a dessert whose very name was slang for the sex act. The nuns and all the other adults were apparently oblivious to the humor.

. . . .

Chocolate Jelly Roll

When you see sliced Chocolate Jelly Roll displayed on a lace paper doily, it looks so pretty you might be fooled into thinking it is hard to make. It isn't! All it takes is patience—and prayer for a deft hand at rolling the thin cake once it is filled.

MAKES 8 TO 10 SERVINGS

2 large eggs, separated
1 cup sifted sugar
10 tablespoons cold water, divided
1 cup sifted all-purpose flour
¼ teaspoon salt
1 teaspoon baking powder
3 tablespoons unsweetened cocoa powder,
   sift cocoa powder into 5 tbsp. water
Powdered sugar
2 cups strawberry jam or preserves

• • • Preheat the oven to 350°F. Beat the egg yolks in a large bowl until thick and light in color. Gradually add the sugar and 5 tablespoons of the water, whisking to blend. Combine the flour, salt, and baking powder; stir into the egg yolk mixture. Sift the cocoa pow-

der into the remaining 5 tablespoons water; mix well. Whisk into the egg mixture.

Beat the egg whites until stiff peaks form. Add the egg whites, a little at a time, to the other ingredients. Spray 2 small or 1 large jelly roll pan with vegetable cooking spray. Line with waxed paper. Spread the batter into the prepared pan(s). Be sure batter is even in pan. Bake 10 to 12 minutes. Turn the cake(s) out onto a slightly damp cloth covered with powdered sugar. Use a sharp knife to cut off any dry edges. Spread the jelly roll(s) with strawberry jam or preserves. Work fast to roll up carefully. Wrap in a cloth. When the cake is cool, roll in powdered sugar. Use a sharp knife to cut jelly roll into 2-inch slices for serving.

—*Brenda Rhodes Miller*

. . . .

Jam Cake

Blackberries are what the recipe calls for, but feel free to substitute your favorite berries and jam. Children will especially love this sweet dessert, so cut small slices and everyone can enjoy it!

MAKES 8 TO 10 SERVINGS

1 cup sugar
⅔ stick butter or margarine
2 cups all-purpose flour
1 teaspoon baking soda
1 teaspoon cinnamon

1 teaspoon allspice

1 cup buttermilk

2 large eggs, separated

1 cup blackberry jam

1 quart fresh blackberries, washed

• • • Preheat the oven to 350°F. Combine the sugar, butter, flour, baking soda, spices, buttermilk, and egg yolks in a large bowl; mix well. Beat the egg whites in a medium bowl until stiff peaks form; fold into the mixture. Fold the jam into the mixture. Pour the batter into a large greased and floured loaf pan. Bake for 35 to 45 minutes or until cake tests done when a wooden toothpick is inserted in the center. Slice when warm and serve with fresh blackberries.

—*Sister M. Consilio Wilson*

Pumpkin Pecan Bundt Cake

At the first hint of fall, church hospitality committees begin planning holiday suppers and holiday gift baskets. This is a great cake to prepare in quantity for a variety of special occasions.

MAKES 24 SERVINGS

1 cup whole pecans

1 (2-layer) package spice cake mix

1 cup canned pumpkin

½ cup salad oil

1 (3-ounce) package vanilla instant
    pudding mix

3 large eggs

1 teaspoon cinnamon

½ cup water

• • • Preheat the oven to 350°F. Grease a Bundt pan and sprinkle with flour. Place whole pecans in bottom of pan (secured to pan with a small piece of butter). Combine the remaining ingredients in a large bowl; mix well. Pour gently into the prepared pan. Bake 40 to 45 minutes or until a wooden toothpick inserted in center comes out clean. Remove from the oven; let cool in pan 10 to 15 minutes. Loosen the center and sides with a plastic spatula. Invert onto a wire rack to cool. Serve with whipped cream or drizzle with icing.

—*Mrs. Willette Bailey*

Pumpkin Roll

Pumpkin Roll freezes well, so make extra for the unexpected meeting at your house of the Ladies' Auxiliary, or whenever friends drop by for a visit.

MAKES 18 TO 20 (½-INCH-THICK) SERVINGS

¾ cup all-purpose flour

1 teaspoon baking powder

1 teaspoon cinnamon

½ teaspoon nutmeg (optional)

Dash of salt

3 large eggs

1 cup sugar

⅔ cup canned pumpkin

1 cup finely chopped pecans

Powdered sugar for dusting

1 cup powdered sugar

1 (8-ounce) package cream cheese

2 tablespoons butter or margarine

½ teaspoon vanilla

• • • Preheat the oven to 375°F. Line a 15-by-10-inch jelly-roll pan or a cookie sheet with sides with waxed paper. Combine the flour, baking powder, cinnamon, nutmeg (if desired), and salt in a large bowl; mix well and set aside. Beat the eggs in a large bowl. Stir in the sugar and the pumpkin. Fold the dry ingredients into the pumpkin mixture, mixing well. Spread the mixture into the lined pan. Sprinkle with the chopped pecans. Bake for 15 minutes. Turn out immediately on a towel or waxed paper sprinkled with a dusting of powdered sugar. Quickly but carefully peel off the waxed paper. Begin at the narrow end and roll the towel and cake together. Refrigerate the cake for 30 minutes. Remove from the refrigerator and unroll. Combine the 1 cup powdered sugar, the cream cheese, butter, and vanilla in a small bowl; mix well. Spread the cream cheese mixture on the inside of the cake. Place the cake on waxed paper, then on aluminum foil. Roll the cake tightly. Then wrap with the waxed paper and foil. Refrigerate for 2 hours before Slice into ½-inch slices

to serve. Roll may be frozen. Thaw for 1 hour, then slice and serve.

NOTE: Could substitute 1½ teaspoons pumpkin pie spice for the cinnamon and nutmeg.

—Mrs. Deloris Agee

. . . .

Pineapple Upside-Down Cake

Quick and easy to make, this cake is not too sweet—just right to serve following Wednesday Night Bible Study or for a weekday dessert after dinner any night.

MAKES 6 TO 8 SERVINGS

½ cup butter or margarine

1 cup firmly packed dark brown sugar

1 (15-ounce) can sliced pineapple

¼ cup whole pecans

3 large eggs, separated

1 cup sugar

5 tablespoons pineapple juice

1 cup all-purpose flour, sifted

1 teaspoon baking powder

Pinch of salt

• • • Preheat the oven to 375°F. Melt the butter in a large cast-iron skillet. Remove the skillet from the heat. Spread the brown sugar evenly over the butter. Drain the pineapple, reserving 5 tablespoons of juice. Lay the pineapple

Church Lady Barbie

MRS. MARTHA COWARDE
Shiloh Baptist Church
Pittsburgh, Pennsylvania

Beverly Mullens, who grew up in the sixties and attended Shiloh Baptist Church in Pittsburgh, Pennsylvania, was inspired every Sunday morning by a wonderful woman named Mrs. Martha Cowarde. "It seemed like Mrs. Cowarde had hundreds of hats," Beverly recalls. "She dazzled me with her gorgeous color-coordinated fashions, always topped with the perfect matching hat."

As a child, Beverly Mullens spent hours in her room sewing clothes for her Barbie dolls. After church on Sunday she rushed home and tried to re-create Mrs. Cowarde's color scheme and the style of that day's hat. "I dressed my Barbies with Mrs. Cowarde in mind."

Fashion extravaganzas are popular in many churches as this photo of Mrs. Anna Chin illustrates.

The Sunday Mrs. Cowarde wore blue, the little girl pulled out her fabrics to fashion an outfit for Barbie that reflected the colors of the sea and sky, designing a flat brimmed boater with curling ribbons in shades of blue that hinted at ocean waves. When Mrs. Cowarde came to church wearing a yellow dress and matching hat, Beverly was inspired to stitch a dress as bright as the sun with a matching cloche hat sporting a ruffle of sharply pointed rays attached to one side.

Sunday after Sunday, Beverly Mullens retired to her sewing studio, which was actually a corner of her bedroom, to make her Barbies the chicest creations on the block. Thanks and unbeknownst to Mrs. Martha Cowarde, she transformed her fashion dolls into perfect church ladies.

slices over the brown sugar. Drop the pecans in the open spaces.

Beat the egg yolks until light in a medium bowl. Stir in the sugar and the reserved pineapple juice. Combine the flour, baking powder, and salt in a medium bowl. Mix with the egg yolk mixture. Beat the egg whites in a medium bowl until stiff peaks form. Fold the whites into the batter. Pour the batter over the pineapple slices. Bake for 30 minutes or until the cake tests done after a wooden toothpick has been inserted. Remove from the oven and turn the cake upside down on a cake plate. Serve with whipped cream or ice cream, if desired.

—*Mrs. Carolyn L. Rhodes*

. . . .

Peach Upside-Down Cake

Waste not, want not is the motto of every true church lady. So, reserve some of the liquid from the canned peaches to mix with whipped cream or nondairy topping for this easy-to-make cake.

MAKES 6 TO 8 SERVINGS

½ cup butter or margarine
1 cup packed dark brown sugar
1 (20-ounce) can sliced peaches
3 large eggs, separated
1 cup sugar
4 tablespoons peach juice
1 cup all-purpose flour

1 teaspoon baking powder
Whipped cream (optional)

• • • Preheat the oven to 350°F. Melt the butter in a large oven-proof skillet. Remove from the heat and add the brown sugar, spreading evenly over bottom of pan and mixing well with the butter. Drain the juice from the peaches, reserving 4 tablespoons. Lay the peach slices over the brown sugar mixture. Beat the egg yolks in a medium bowl. Add the sugar and the reserved peach juice. Sift together the flour and baking powder. Add to the egg yolk mixture. Beat the egg whites until stiff peaks form. Fold into the batter and mix well. Pour the batter over the peaches; spread evenly. Bake about 40 to 60 minutes, or until a wooden toothpick comes out clean. Remove from the oven and turn cake out onto a flat serving dish. Serve with whipped cream, if desired.

—*Mrs. Beulah Hughes*

. . . .

Tangerine Cake

Tastes like sunshine! This recipe came from a choir member in Florida who prides herself on baking with the sweetest, ripest, and freshest fruit available to her.

MAKES 10 TO 12 SERVINGS

5 large eggs, separated
1¼ cups sugar

¼ cup tangerine juice (about 1 large tangerine)
1¼ cups all-purpose flour
1 teaspoon baking powder
Tangerine Filling (page 185)

• • •Preheat the oven to 350°F. Beat the egg yolks in a large bowl. Add the sugar and beat until smooth. Stir in the juice, mixing well. Sift together the flour and baking powder in a medium bowl. Gradually add to the liquid batter; mix well. Beat the egg whites in a medium bowl until light peaks form. Fold the egg whites into the batter. Spoon the batter into two greased and floured, round (9-inch) cake pans. Bake for 40 minutes. Cool on wire racks. Remove from pans and spread Tangerine Filling between layers and on top of cake.

—*Carol Martin*

Italian Cream Cake

When volunteers are asked to bring desserts for the Repast following a funeral, this rich cake is always one that a close family friend bakes. To keep it from disappearing too quickly, you may want to slice it extra thin.

MAKES 16 TO 18 SERVINGS

½ cup shortening
1 stick butter or margarine
2 cups sugar
5 eggs, separated

2 cups all-purpose flour
1 teaspoon baking soda
½ teaspoon salt
1 cup buttermilk
1 teaspoon vanilla
1 cup chopped pecans
1 cup shredded coconut

• • •Preheat the oven to 350°F. Cream the shortening, butter, and sugar in a large bowl. Add the 5 egg yolks, one at a time, beating well after each addition. Add the flour and the remaining dry ingredients. Stir in the buttermilk and the vanilla; blend well. Fold in the pecans and coconut. Beat egg whites until stiff peaks form. Fold into the batter. Spoon into three well-greased and floured round cake pans. Bake for 25 to 30 minutes. Cool on racks and then spread the Cream Cheese Frosting between layers and over top and sides.

CREAM CHEESE FROSTING
1 stick butter or margarine
1 (8-ounce) package cream cheese
1 (16-ounce) package powdered sugar
1 teaspoon vanilla
1 cup chopped pecans

Cream the butter and cream cheese at room temperature in a large bowl. Add the powdered sugar and the vanilla, mixing until smooth. Stir in the chopped pecans.

—*Mrs. Deloris Agee*

Chocolate Chip Cake

If you're a person who never tires of chocolate, this cake will make you jump for joy. Try to keep in mind that greed is one of the seven deadly sins.

MAKES 12 SERVINGS

1 package yellow cake mix

1 (3-ounce) package instant vanilla pudding

⅔ cup vegetable oil

1 cup water

3 large eggs, at room temperature

1 (4-ounce) bar German chocolate, grated and divided

1 (6-ounce) package semisweet chocolate chips

3 tablespoons powdered sugar

• • • Preheat the oven to 350°F. Grease and flour a 13-by-9-inch baking pan. Combine the cake mix, pudding mix, oil, water, and eggs in a large bowl. Blend with mixer until moistened. Beat for two minutes at medium speed. Fold in half the grated chocolate and the chocolate chips. Pour into the baking pan. Bake for 40 to 45 minutes. Remove from the oven. Combine the remaining grated chocolate and the powdered sugar in a small bowl. Sprinkle on top of the hot cake.

—*Mrs. Deloris Agee*

Sock-It-to-Me Cake

This version of the popular not-quite-from-scratch cake is so easy to make you'll want to bring one whenever your church hosts a dinner for a visiting church.

MAKES 20 SERVINGS

1 (2-layer) package yellow cake mix

½ cup water

½ cup vegetable oil

½ cup sour cream

4 large eggs

1 (3-ounce) package instant vanilla pudding

½ cup sugar

1 tablespoon cinnamon

1½ cups chopped pecans

• • • Preheat the oven to 350°F. Combine the cake mix, water, oil, sour cream, eggs, and pudding mix in a large bowl; mix well. Spoon half of the batter into a greased and floured 13-by-9-inch cake pan. Combine the sugar, cinnamon, and pecans in a small bowl. Spoon half the sugar mixture over the batter. Top with the remaining batter, then the remaining sugar mixture. Bake 50 minutes, then test for doneness with a wooden toothpick. Remove from oven and cool on a wire rack for about 15 minutes. Remove cake from pan onto a serving platter.

—*Mrs. Nishia L. Brack*

Cream Cheese Pound Cake

Pound cake fans will have a new favorite when you serve this to them at the church picnic. Bake it on a cool day and slice it in advance, wrap carefully, and freeze it. That way, you won't have to turn your oven on in the heat of summer.

MAKES 12 SERVINGS

1½ cups butter or margarine
1 (8-ounce) package cream cheese
3 cups sugar
Dash of salt
1½ teaspoons vanilla
6 large eggs
3 cups all-purpose flour, sifted

• • • Preheat the oven to 325°F. Cream the butter, cream cheese, and sugar in a large bowl until light and fluffy. Add salt and vanilla. Mix well. Add eggs, one at a time, beating well after each addition. Stir in the flour. Spoon mixture into greased and floured 10-inch tube pan and bake for about 1½ hours. The top should be crusty.

—Mrs. Doris Hicks

Sour Cream Pound Cake

Nothing is quite as good as rich, homemade pound cake. This one just about cries out for pride of place at the Pastor's Anniversary supper.

MAKES 24 SERVINGS

2 sticks butter or margarine
½ cup shortening
2½ to 3 cups sugar
5 large eggs
3¼ cups cake flour
¼ teaspoon nutmeg
½ teaspoon baking powder
Dash of salt
1 cup sour cream
1 teaspoon vanilla

• • • Preheat the oven to 325°F. Grease and flour a springform cake pan. Cream the butter and shortening in a large bowl; gradually add the sugar. Add the eggs, one at a time, beating after each addition. Combine the flour, nutmeg, baking powder, and the salt in a large bowl. Stir the flour mixture into the creamed mixture alternately with the sour cream; mix well. Stir in the vanilla. Pour into the prepared pan. Bake for 1½ hours or until golden brown on top. Cool slightly in the pan. Remove the outside of the pan. Cool completely.

NOTE: If desired, sift powdered sugar

over the top of the cake before serving or add a dollop of vanilla ice cream to each serving.

—*Mrs. Deloris Agee*

. . . .

Lemon Coconut Pound Cake

Lemon and coconut make such beautiful music together, this cake should be served at Appreciation Day for the Senior Choir. No doubt at least a few of the older members remember this recipe when it was made with a pound of butter instead of the butter-and-cream-cheese mixture featured here—just one example of how recipes change over the generations.

MAKES 16 SERVINGS

1¼ cups butter

1 (8-ounce) package cream cheese

3 cups sugar

1 tablespoon lemon juice

2 tablespoons vanilla extract

½ teaspoon coconut extract

3 cups all-purpose flour

⅛ teaspoon salt

6 large eggs

1 cup flaked coconut, divided

1 cup powdered sugar

1 tablespoon butter

2 tablespoons lemon juice

2 teaspoons lemon peel

1 teaspoon coconut extract

• • • Preheat the oven to 325°F. Cream the butter, cream cheese, and sugar in a large bowl until light and fluffy. Add the lemon juice, the vanilla, and the ½ teaspoon coconut extract. Sift together the flour and salt in a medium bowl. Alternate adding the eggs and the flour mixture into the creamed mixture, mixing well after each addition. Fold in ¾ cup of the coconut. Coat a 10-inch tube pan with oil and then flour. Pour the batter into the pan. Bake for 1½ to 2 hours or until golden brown. Cool the cake in the pan for 10 to 15 minutes, then invert onto a serving plate.

Combine the powdered sugar, butter, lemon juice, lemon peel, and coconut extract in a small bowl. Mix well. Pour over the cooled cake. Top the cake with the remaining ¼ cup coconut.

—*Mrs. Sandra E. Thomas*

. . . .

Chocolate Pound Cake

After Tuesday Prayer Warriors gather for their noontime service, they still need to eat lunch. Chocolate Pound Cake is the perfect ending to their meal. What could be better than combining two great tastes?

MAKES 10 TO 12 SERVINGS

2 sticks butter or margarine

½ cup shortening

3 cups sugar

5 large eggs

6 tablespoons unsweetened cocoa powder

3 cups all-purpose flour

1 teaspoon baking powder

Pinch of salt

1 cup milk

1 tablespoon vanilla

Powdered sugar

• • • Preheat the oven to 325°F. Cream the butter, shortening, sugar, and eggs in a large mixing bowl. Sift the cocoa powder, flour, baking powder, and salt in another large bowl. Combine the milk and vanilla. Add the dry ingredients and milk mixture alternately to the creamed mixture until well blended. Spoon into a greased and floured large Bundt pan. Bake for 1 hour 15 minutes, or until a wooden toothpick inserted in the center comes out clean. Cool slightly. Remove from pan. Sift powdered sugar over the cake or add frosting or a glaze.

—Mrs. Carol Preston

. . . .

Red Velvet Pound Cake

This has been the contributor's official family birthday cake for the past twenty years. Special church friends have been known to request it for their birthdays as well . . . with mixed results!

3 sticks butter or margarine

3 cups sugar

8 large eggs

2 teaspoons vanilla extract

1 ounce red food coloring

3 cups cake flour

½ cup sifted unsweetened cocoa powder

¼ teaspoon salt

1 cup milk

Pineapple Cream Cheese Frosting
    (see page 176)

• • • Preheat the oven to 325°F. Cream the butter and sugar in a large bowl until light and fluffy. Add the eggs, one at a time, beating well after each addition. Stir in the vanilla and food coloring. Combine the flour, cocoa, and salt in a large bowl. Stir into the creamed mixture, one cup at a time, alternating with ⅓ cup milk until all the dry ingredients and milk have been incorporated. Pour the batter into a greased and floured tube pan. Bake for about 65 to 75 minutes or until cake tests done when checked with a long wooden pick. Turn cake out onto a wire rack; let cool. Frost with Pineapple Cream Cheese Frosting.

—Mrs. Brenda Rhodes Miller

. . . .

Silence is Golden

MRS. BARBARA WINFIELD
Second Baptist Church
Burlington, New Jersey

Mr. and Mrs. Winfield ushered in the balcony of Second Baptist Church," recollects Michele Brown. "They were the cutest couple! Mrs. Winfield was taller than her husband, and she *barely* made five-foot five. But he had such a big personality he might as well have been seven feet tall! Neither of them paid any attention to the height difference.

"My friends and I sat together in the balcony for eleven-o'clock service, talking in whispers, making faces, and giggling as if we'd forgotten we were in church. Most Sundays, Mrs. Winfield just glared at us, her sweet, gentle little face suddenly stern.

"Holding a gloved finger to her lips in the universal sign for silence, Mrs. Winfield stood our silliness as long as she could. When one of us actually had the temerity to laugh out loud, Mrs. Winfield decided enough was enough.

"With laserlike precision, she identified the ringleader, who all too often was me. Like a stealth missile, Mrs. Winfield would home in on me with her teeth clenched. Then she'd lean over, and in a voice only God and I could hear, she would say, 'I asked you to stop talking. I shall not ask you again.' This admonition was followed by a pinch of unspeakably painful proportions. Mrs. Winfield had the uncanny ability to find the softest, most tender part of my upper arm. Like a wrathful lobster, she latched on to the spot with fingers that had the power of a pair of white-hot pliers. She stunned me with that pinch until I could neither speak nor hear, whimpering as tears of fear rolled down my cheeks.

"And, as if it were not bad enough that the wrath of God had fallen on me in the guise of Mrs.Winfield's legendary pinch, worse yet was the knowledge that my mother, sitting downstairs in the choir stand, had seen it all. Certain death loomed in my mind."

Mrs. Winfield still chairs the Junior Usher Board at Second Baptist Church according to Michele Brown.

Sweet Potato Pound Cake

The lowly sweet potato may be one of the most versatile items in God's creation. Here, it gives pound cake a beautiful color and a new flavor.

MAKES 16 TO 18 SERVINGS

1 cup butter or margarine, softened

2 cups sugar

4 large eggs

*2½ cups cooked mashed sweet potatoes
    (about 2½ pounds sweet potatoes)*

3 cups all-purpose flour

2 teaspoons baking powder

1 teaspoon baking soda

1 teaspoon ground cinnamon

½ teaspoon ground nutmeg

¼ teaspoon salt

1 teaspoon vanilla extract

½ cup flaked coconut

1 cup chopped pecans

• • • Preheat the oven to 350°F. Cream the butter in a large bowl. Add the sugar gradually, beating well. Add the eggs, one at a time, beating well after each addition. Add the sweet potatoes, beating well. Combine the flour, baking powder, baking soda, cinnamon, nutmeg, and salt in a large bowl. Add the flour mixture to the creamed mixture gradually, beating well after each addition. The batter will be stiff. Stir in the vanilla, coconut, and pecans. Spoon the batter into a well-greased 10-inch tube pan. Bake for 1 hour and 15 minutes or until the cake tests done when a wire cake tester is inserted in the middle. Cool the cake in the pan for 15 minutes. Remove from the pan and let cool completely.

—*Mrs. Virginia Strong*

Red Velvet Cake

You have to be in the right mood to make a Red Velvet Cake. Only make it for someone you love. The real test of affection is when you bake one and it fails. Nearly proof positive your heart isn't in the right place.

MAKES 12 TO 16 SERVINGS

1½ cups sugar

1½ cups vegetable oil

2 large eggs

3 tablespoons unsweetened cocoa powder

2½ cups self-rising flour

1 cup buttermilk

1 teaspoon vanilla

1 ounce red food coloring

1 teaspoon vinegar

1 teaspoon baking soda

Frosting (see below)

1 cup coarsely chopped pecans (optional)

• • • Preheat the oven to 350°F. Cream the sugar and oil in a large bowl. Add the eggs, mixing well. Combine the cocoa powder and flour. Add the buttermilk and flour mixture alternately to the creamed mixture, mixing well after each addition. Stir in the vanilla and food coloring. Beat well. Combine the vinegar and baking soda; add to the batter. Beat well. Pour in three well-greased and floured, 8-inch, round cake pans. Bake 30 to 35 minutes. Remove from the oven and cool. Layer with frosting and cover the top and sides. Decorate with pecans, if desired.

FROSTING

1 (8-ounce) package cream cheese, softened
1 stick butter or margarine
2 (16-ounce) packages powdered sugar
1 teaspoon vanilla

Cream the cream cheese and butter in a medium bowl with an electric mixer. Slowly add the powdered sugar until well mixed. Stir in the vanilla.

—*Mrs. Bessie Brazley*

A beaming Mrs. Willette Bailey shows off her new winter hat, and a beautifully laid table.

Sweet Potato Cake

For just about forty years, Ms. Willette Bailey has been going to St. Charles Catholic Church in Harlem. She's not Catholic. In fact, she is and has always been a Congregationalist, a Nazarene. But her home church is way out in Brooklyn, and since she lives on 140th Street and St. Charles is at 141st near Seventh Avenue, she goes to St. Charles to worship. The church is only about a block and a half from her house, which means she can walk there, no matter what the weather.

Ms. Bailey often says, "There's only one God, and he's the same one no matter where you go. It's the same God everywhere, no matter where you pray."

MAKES 10 TO 12 SERVINGS

2 cups all-purpose flour
2¼ teaspoons baking powder
½ teaspoon baking soda

½ *teaspoon salt*

1 *teaspoon cinnamon*

1 *teaspoon nutmeg*

½ *teaspoon cloves*

2 *cups sugar*

1 *cup peanut oil*

4 *large eggs, separated*

1 ½ *cups grated raw sweet potato*

1 *cup chopped pecans or sliced almonds*

⅓ *cup hot water*

Powdered sugar (optional)

• • • Preheat the oven to 350°F. Stir together the flour, baking powder, baking soda, salt, cinnamon, nutmeg, and cloves in a large bowl; set aside. Combine the sugar and peanut oil in another large bowl. Beat in the egg yolks, one at a time. Add the grated sweet potato and chopped nuts. Add the dry ingredients alternately with the hot water, mixing thoroughly. Beat the egg whites in a medium bowl until stiff peaks form. Fold into the sweet potato batter using a spatula. Pour the batter into a greased and floured 10-inch tube pan. Bake for 1 hour or until the cake springs back when touched and begins to leave the sides of the pan. Cool in the pan 10 minutes. Remove from the pan and cool completely. If desired, sprinkle with powdered sugar just before serving.

NOTE: Cake can be baked in a loaf pan, sliced, and served with cream cheese.

—*Ms. Willette Bailey*

Fruity Cake

All the fruit in this recipe makes for a truly delicious cake that should be shared for maximum enjoyment. Why not bake one for the First Lady's Tea? Surely, the Pastor's wife would welcome such a treat.

MAKES 12 TO 15 SERVINGS

3 *cups all-purpose flour*

2 *cups sugar*

1 *teaspoon salt*

1 *teaspoon cinnamon*

1 *teaspoon baking soda*

3 *large eggs, beaten*

1 ½ *cups salad oil*

1 ½ *teaspoon vanilla*

1 *(8-ounce) can crushed pineapple, undrained*

1 *cup chopped pecans (plus additional for garnish, optional)*

2 *cups chopped banana*

• • • Preheat the oven to 350°F. Combine the flour, sugar, salt, cinnamon, and baking soda in a large bowl. Add the eggs and the oil. Mix well. Stir in the vanilla, pineapple, pecans, and banana. Spoon into a greased and floured Bundt pan. Bake for 1 hour and 20 minutes. Cool for 10 minutes before removing from pan. Cool completely before frosting.

½ *(8-ounce) package cream cheese, softened*

¼ *cup butter or margarine*

½ *(16-ounce) package powdered sugar*

½ *teaspoon vanilla*

½ *cup chopped pecans (optional)*

Combine the cream cheese and the butter in a large bowl, mixing until smooth. Add the powdered sugar and the vanilla, beating until light and fluffy. Spread on the sides and top of cake. Sprinkle additional pecans on top if desired.

—*adapted from* Family and Friends Favorite Recipes

. . . .

Gingerbread

Just the smell of homemade gingerbread brings comfort and memories of Youth Choir practice. It always ended with a sweet reward, gingerbread in the winter and ice cream in the summer.

MAKES 18 SERVINGS

1 cup butter or margarine

½ *cup sugar*

2 eggs

1 cup molasses

1 teaspoon cinnamon

1 ½ teaspoons ginger

½ *teaspoon salt*

1 teaspoon baking soda

1 cup boiling water

3 cups all-purpose flour

1 teaspoon baking powder

1 cup golden raisins (optional)

Frosting (optional; recipe follows)

• • • Preheat the oven to 350°F. Cream the butter and the sugar in a large bowl. Add the eggs, mixing well. Add the molasses, cinnamon, ginger, and salt; mix well. Dissolve the baking soda in the boiling water. Add to the creamed mixture. Sift in the flour and the baking powder, mixing well. Stir in the raisins, if desired. Pour the mixture into a greased 3-quart oblong baking pan. Bake for 40 minutes or until done. Add frosting, if desired, while cake is still warm.

FROSTING

1 cup powdered sugar

4 tablespoons cream

¼ *teaspoon vanilla*

Combine all the ingredients in a small bowl. Mix well.

—*Ms. Willette Bailey*

. . . .

The Joy of Helping

MRS. LA RUTH PRYOR
Barraque Street Missionary Baptist Church
Pine Bluff, Arkansas

Her voice is soft like a Delta breeze. Gentle and unassuming, Mrs. La Ruth Pryor nonetheless displays a courtly manner, which speaks of the influence her great-aunt and mother provided during her childhood in Forest City, Arkansas.

An only child, Mrs. Pryor wanted a broad kinship network for her own two children. She created one by cooking for and encouraging frequent, big, communal dinners that included several other church families.

According to her son, "She has such an even disposition, she never puts on airs. She's very down-to-earth, but she always knows exactly how things should be done."

All these qualities make her effective on the Social Committee of her church. This committee is responsible for every meal provided at church, including the food served after funerals. As Mrs. Pryor modestly admits, French dimples twinkling on both sides of her smile, "We do everything. We're involved in some form or fashion with any meal done at church or through church. We've even started to do some weddings!"

The Social Committee also used to "do" several teas throughout the year, but now that teas have fallen out of fashion at the church, its big event is in February. That's when Mrs. Pryor and the Social Committee prepare a special soul food potluck. One Sunday, in honor of Black History Month, the entire committee dresses in African attire and presents a lavish buffet of soul food dishes, along with other items, for the congregation.

Currently president of the Missionary Society, Mrs. Pryor originally joined because she wanted to learn more about

A wedding reception held in the church basement with sparkling cider standing in for the traditional champagne toasts. Generous church ladies lent their own candlesticks and glasses for the celebration.

the Bible. She says, "Our minister is a great teacher, who believes in sharing the Word of God, and that's very important to me."

The membership of the Missionary Society is divided, usually by age, into circles. These circles meet from one to four times a month to study mission work and the Bible, and each circle has its own lesson books, a chairperson, and teachers.

Each circle includes about seventy-five women and has its own name, such as Willing Workers, United Circle, and the Progressive Women. This year, the theme for all the circles is prayer.

In addition to leading the Missionary Society, Mrs. Pryor, a retired high school teacher, has also done a great deal of Sunday school work, especially with nine- to eleven-year-old children.

When asked why she devotes so much time and energy to church work, she says, "It is a joy to help someone else in need. It makes you forget your own trials and tribulations. I love helping people."

Rumor has it that Mrs. Pryor not only performs great service to her church and her fellowman; she also makes a fabulous German chocolate cake, a recipe for which appears in this book on page 12.

Nut Gingerbread

If you like nuts, you'll really like Nut Gingerbread. It has a special taste that transports adults and children alike to the holy land of Bible stories and the fabled spice routes.

MAKES 12 TO 15 SERVINGS

2 cups all-purpose flour

1 teaspoon baking soda

½ teaspoon salt

1 teaspoon ginger

1½ cups packed dark brown sugar

½ cup molasses

¼ cup butter or margarine, melted

1 large egg, well beaten

1 cup milk

5 tablespoons chopped pecans

2½ tablespoons dark brown sugar

• • • Preheat the oven to 350°F. Sift the flour, then sift with the baking soda, salt, and ginger in a medium bowl. Combine the 1½ cups brown sugar, molasses, butter, and egg in a large bowl, mixing well. Add the dry ingredients alternately with the milk; beat until well blended. Pour into a well-greased 13-by-9-inch baking pan. Sprinkle with the nuts and the 2½ tablespoons brown sugar. Bake for 30 to 35 minutes. Serve warm with a dollop of whipped cream if desired.

—*Mrs. Melanie Shelwood*

Fresh Apple Cake

When apples are sweet and plentiful, use them to make this delightful cake. Take it to the next church meeting and get ready for the compliments.

MAKES 10 TO 12 SERVINGS

2 cups sugar
1¼ cups vegetable oil
3 large eggs
2½ cups all-purpose flour
1 teaspoon baking soda
2 teaspoons baking powder
1 teaspoon salt
1 tablespoon vanilla
3 cups chopped Granny Smith apples
    (about 2 medium), peeled
1 cup finely chopped pecans
Sauce (recipe follows)

• • • Preheat the oven to 350°F. Combine the sugar and the next seven ingredients in a large bowl; mix well. Fold in the apples and the nuts. Pour the mixture into a 10-inch Bundt pan. Bake for 1 hour. Pour the Sauce over the hot cake and let stand until cool. Remove from pan.

SAUCE
1 stick butter or margarine
½ cup buttermilk
1 cup sugar

½ teaspoon baking soda
1 teaspoon vanilla

Combine all the ingredients in a medium saucepan. Bring to a boil and continue to boil for 10 minutes.

—Mrs. Lucille Battle

Apricot Nectarine Cake

This light and luscious cake is a perfect church supper summertime dessert. Fold the egg whites with care. Otherwise you may flatten the final product.

MAKES 16 TO 18 SERVINGS

4 large eggs, separated
1 package yellow cake mix
¾ cup vegetable oil
¾ cup canned apricot nectar
3 teaspoons lemon extract
¼ cup lemon juice
1 cup powdered sugar

• • • Preheat the oven to 325°F. Beat the egg yolks in a large bowl. Add the cake mix, oil, apricot nectar, and lemon extract, mixing well. Beat the egg whites in a medium bowl until stiff peaks form. Fold the egg whites into the batter. Pour into a greased and floured tube pan. Bake for 50 minutes or until the cake tests done. Combine the lemon juice and powdered sugar in a small bowl. Drizzle over warm cake. Cool the cake before removing from pan.

—*Dr. Willie Creagh Bolden*

....

Mississippi Mud Cake

Whether the Nile, the Jordan, or the Mississippi River, it is the rich, fertile mud that makes for bountiful crops. The only resemblance this cake has to mud is the deep, dark chocolate color. Nothing but good.

MAKES 12 TO 15 SERVINGS

1 cup butter or margarine, softened

2 cups sugar

2 tablespoons unsweetened cocoa powder

4 large eggs

1 teaspoon vanilla

1½ cups all-purpose flour

1½ cups coarsely chopped walnuts

1½ cups flaked coconut

• • • Preheat the oven to 350°F. Combine the butter, sugar, cocoa, eggs, and vanilla in a large bowl; mix until creamy. Add the flour, nuts, and coconut. Mix thoroughly. Pour into a greased and floured 13-by-9-inch baking pan. Bake for 40 to 45 minutes. Cool before serv-

ing. If desired, serve warm with ice cream or a dollop of whipped cream.

—*Family and Friends Favorite Recipes*

....

Fruitcake

The contributor's mother, who taught the New Members Class, always had her husband, who chaired the Administrative Board, stir the batter for her because it was so heavy with fruit.

MAKES 3 (8-BY-4-INCH) LOAF CAKES

1 pound butter or margarine

2 cups sugar

10 large eggs, separated

3 cups all-purpose flour (reserving 1 cup to coat fruit)

1 teaspoon baking soda

1 cup pineapple juice

1½ pounds candied pineapple

1 pound candied red and green cherries

¼ pound citron

¼ pound orange peel

¼ pound lemon peel

4 cups chopped pecans

½ cup whiskey or wine

2 teaspoons vanilla

• • • Preheat the oven to 325°F. Cream the butter and sugar in a large bowl until fluffy. Add the egg yolks. Sift together 2 cups of the flour and baking soda. Add to the creamed mixture along with the pineapple juice. Use the remaining 1 cup flour to coat the fruit in a separate bowl. Add the floured fruit and the nuts to the batter. Beat the egg whites until stiff. Fold the egg whites, whiskey, and vanilla into the batter until well mixed. Pour into greased loaf pans. Bake for about 1½ hours or until cake tests done when a toothpick is inserted.

NOTE: Dates and raisins may also be added to the batter. If desired, dissolve one cup sugar in one cup hot water and glaze cake with sugar-and-water mixture during the last few minutes of baking. You can also garnish the top with additional pineapples, cherries, and nuts before baking.

—*Mrs. Carolyn L. Rhodes*

Mrs. G's Rum Cake

If you're concerned about the cup of rum in this recipe, don't worry. The alcohol evaporates in the baking, leaving behind only the flavor of the rum. Rum Cake freezes perfectly and makes a welcomed holiday gift.

MAKES 16 SERVINGS

1 cup chopped pecans
1 (18-ounce) package yellow cake mix
1 (3-ounce) package vanilla instant
   pudding mix
4 large eggs
½ cup cold water
½ cup cooking oil
1 cup dark rum, divided
¼ pound butter
¼ cup water
1 cup sugar
Whole maraschino cherries
Sweetened whipped cream
Seedless green grapes
Powdered sugar

• • • Preheat the oven to 325°F. Grease and flour two 10-inch cake pans or one 12-inch Bundt pan. Sprinkle the pecans on the bottom of pan(s). Prepare the cake mix in a large bowl according to the directions on the package, using the pudding mix, 4 eggs, cold water, cooking oil, and ½ cup of the rum. Pour the batter over the nuts in the pan(s). Bake for 1 hour. Cool slightly on a wire rack. Remove from the pan(s). Cool on a serving plate.

To make the glaze, melt the butter in a large saucepan. Combine the ¼ cup water and the sugar. Slowly stir the mixture into the butter. Boil for 5 minutes, stirring constantly. Remove from heat, stir in the remaining ½ cup of rum. Pierce the cooled cake with a fork several times and slowly pour the glaze over it. Allow the cake to cool completely. Decorate the top with whole maraschino cherries and sweetened whipped cream. Serve with seedless green grapes dusted with powdered sugar.

—*Zöe M. Isaac Gadsden (along with Dr. Willie Creagh Bolden's recipe)*

7 UP® Cake

You can substitute your favorite soft drink for the 7 UP® called for in the recipe. If you don't frost this cake, you can safely serve it to children because it won't make a mess. You could serve it as cupcakes after Sunday school class.

MAKES 12 TO 15 SERVINGS

3 sticks butter or margarine, softened
3½ cups sugar
6 large eggs
3 cups all-purpose flour
3 teaspoons lemon extract
¾ cup 7 UP®
Cooking spray

• • • Preheat the oven to 325°F. Cream the butter and sugar in a large bowl until well mixed. Add the eggs, flour, lemon extract, and 7 UP®; mix well. Spoon mixture into a 10-inch tube pan coated with cooking spray. Bake for 1 hour and 15 minutes or until cake tests done when a wooden toothpick is inserted and comes out clean. Add frosting, if desired.

—Mrs. Philonese Thompson

Swiss Chocolate Dump Cake

This may be the easiest cake you'll ever bake. The Teen Ministry might enjoy giving it a try for their Friday night fellowship.

MAKES 12 SERVINGS

1 (20-ounce) can crushed pineapple
    with juice, undrained
1 (20-ounce) can cherry pie filling
1 package moist deluxe Swiss chocolate cake
    mix (Duncan Hines)
1 cup chopped pecans
½ cup butter or margarine, cut into
    thin slices

• • • Preheat the oven to 350°F. Pour the pineapple with juice into an ungreased 13-by-9-inch cake pan. Spread evenly over pan. Spoon the pie filling over the pineapple; spread evenly. Sprinkle the cake mix evenly over the cherry layer. Top with the pecans. Dot the surface with the butter slices. Bake for 50 to 55 minutes or until set. Serve warm or at room temperature.

—Mrs. Diana R. Weekes

Mother Loved Sunday School

MRS. CAROLYN L. RHODES
Toulminville-Warren UMC
Mobile, Alabama

She didn't sing in the choir, and she never ushered. She didn't play the piano or cook for church gatherings. Yet mother was the quintessential church lady. She loved Sunday worship and was a faithful member of the pew, participating every Sunday morning. Mother knew all the words to all the hymns, and sang them with gusto.

Her passion was Sunday school. Some of my earliest memories are of going to Sunday school with my mother, who taught the nursery class when I was small because I would cry if she left me.

When I learned to read, she told me I was a big girl and could go to my Sunday school class without her. Then, she returned to her adult class, where they studied the Bible and learned to be Christians in a modern world.

Later, when my youngest sister cried as I had done at her age, Mother insisted that I accompany my sister to Sunday school. Of course, I did as I was told and wound up teaching the nursery class myself for ten years.

Aside and apart from making sure her daughters provided service to the church, my mother encouraged us by her example. Unless we were deathly ill, she expected us to attend church each week, as she did herself.

In addition to her Christian witness, Mother was the most stylish of church ladies. Her curly black hair was always fashionably set. She wore the prettiest clothes, usually in bright colors that flattered her neat little figure. She was fond of hats but

In 1956, Mrs. Carolyn Rhodes and four-year-old daughter, Brenda.

drew the line at wearing those big elaborate ones, declaring that she wanted to wear the hat, not have the hat wear her.

During even the hottest Alabama summers, her crisp, pastel linen suits never wilted into sweaty wads as my own clothing did. She seems to me the perfect example of a church lady in word, deed, and demeanor.

When last we went to church together, my mother was fragile from months of chemotherapy. It was an unseasonably hot day and to keep her from being bothered by the heat, I fanned and fanned, working myself into a sweat as I tried with all my might to make her comfortable, to make her well.

Pecan Sticks

Another individual-serving dessert that looks especially nice when served on a fancy cut-glass cake stand. Good for church teas and receptions.

MAKES 16 SERVINGS

½ cup butter

⅔ cup sugar

2 large eggs

½ cup milk

1 cup finely chopped pecans, divided

1½ cups all-purpose flour

½ teaspoon salt

2 teaspoons baking powder

1 teaspoon vanilla

Brown Sugar Frosting (page 176)

• • • Preheat the oven to 350°F. Cream the butter and sugar in a large bowl. Add the eggs and vanilla, beating until well mixed. Stir in the milk and ¾ cup of the pecans. Combine the flour, salt, and baking powder in a bowl; sift together. Mix with the creamed mixture, beating thoroughly. Spoon the batter into greased finger-roll or corn-muffin pans. Bake for 20 minutes. Remove from the pan and cool on a rack. When cool, spread with Brown Sugar Frosting, or another frosting of your choice, mixed with the remaining ¼ cup pecans.

Carrot Cake

A textured, hearty cake that manages to sneak a few vitamins in while no one is looking. What a treat for the Young Adults' Ministry to share over coffee.

MAKES 10 SERVINGS

2 cups sugar

1½ cups vegetable oil

4 large eggs

2 cups all-purpose flour

2 teaspoons baking powder

2 teaspoons baking soda

1 teaspoon salt

1 teaspoon ground cinnamon

¾ teaspoon ground nutmeg

3 cups finely grated peeled carrots
   (about 1 pound)

½ cup chopped pecans

½ cup golden raisins

Frosting (recipe follows)

• • • Preheat the oven to 350°F. Lightly grease and flour 1 (10-inch) tube pan. Beat the sugar and vegetable oil in a large bowl until well mixed. Add the eggs, one at a time, beating well after each addition. Sift the flour, baking powder, baking soda, salt, cinnamon, and nutmeg into a large bowl, mixing well. Add to the creamed mixture. Stir in the carrots, pecans, and raisins.

Pour the batter into the prepared pan. Bake for about 1 hour or until cake tests done through center. Cool in the pan for 15 minutes. Turn the cake onto a wire rack and cool completely. (Cake can be made one day ahead. Wrap tightly in plastic and store at room temperature.)

Place the cake on a platter. Spread the frosting on sides and top of cake. Make decorative swirls in the frosting using a spatula. (Frosting can be prepared two days ahead.) Cover the cake and refrigerate. Serve cake cold or at room temperature.

FROSTING

4 cups powdered sugar

2 (8-ounce) packages cream cheese,
   room temperature

½ cup (1 stick) unsalted butter, room
   temperature

4 teaspoons vanilla extract

Milk as needed

Combine all the ingredients in a medium bowl; beat well with an electric mixer until smooth and creamy. Add milk if needed for spreading consistency.

—Ms. Wendy Johnson

Tropical Icebox Fruitcake

Make this sweet, gooey cake for Men's Day, and everyone with a sweet tooth will ask you for the recipe.

MAKES 20 SERVINGS

1 (8-ounce) box gingersnaps, crushed

1 pound fresh coconut

1 (10-ounce) jar maraschino cherries,
   well drained

1 pound chopped pecans

10 ounces sweetened condensed milk

1 pound seedless white raisins

• • • Combine all the ingredients in a large bowl; mix well. Line a loaf pan with waxed paper. Pack the cake mixture firmly in the pan. Cover tightly, and refrigerate overnight. Slice very thin and serve with orange sherbet.

—*Ms. Melanie Shelwood*

ter is stiff, then drop about 2 teaspoons each on a greased baking sheet. Bake for 10 minutes. Serve with Fruit Sauce.

—*Mrs. Brenda Rhodes Miller*

Lemon Mountains

Before you bake Lemon Mountains for church members who are sick and shut-in, make sure none have dietary restrictions that would keep them from enjoying these pretty little sweets. You wouldn't want to have to eat them all by yourself, or, would you?

MAKES 2 DOZEN

½ cup butter or margarine
¾ cup sugar
2 large eggs
3 cups cake flour
3 teaspoons baking powder
¼ teaspoon salt
Grated rind of 2 lemons
Juice of 1 lemon
Fruit Sauce (page 174)

• • • Preheat the oven to 325°F. Cream the butter and sugar in a large bowl. Add the eggs, one at a time, beating well after each addition. Sift together the flour, baking powder, and salt in a medium bowl. Add the dry ingredients to the creamed mixture slowly, then add the lemon rind and the juice. Beat well so the bat-

Strawberry Shortcake

Pastel dresses and fancy straw hats worn to an afternoon church program say summer is here and so does the quintessential summer dessert—strawberry shortcake.

MAKES 6 SERVINGS

1 quart strawberries, cleaned and sliced
¼ cup sugar
2 cups all-purpose flour
4 teaspoons baking powder
Pinch of salt
2 tablespoons butter or margarine, softened
½ cup milk
Butter or margarine
Whipped cream (optional)

• • • Preheat the oven to 450°F. Combine the strawberries and sugar in a small bowl; mix well and set aside. Combine the flour, baking powder, and salt in a large bowl. Add the butter, working it into the flour mixture with your hands. Add the milk, mixing well. Place the flour mixture on a lightly floured board and pat it into two large (9-inch) cakes. Place one cake in a well-greased, round 9-inch baking pan.

Lay the other cake on top of it. Bake for 15 to 20 minutes. Remove from the oven and cut the cake into six portions, similar to cutting a pie. Break each of the six portions in half horizontally. Liberally butter the insides and then fill with strawberries. Replace top. Add strawberries over the top and whipped cream, if desired.

NOTE: Peaches or raspberries may be substituted for the strawberries.

—Ms. Beverly Crandall

. . . .

Old-Fashioned Strawberry Shortcake

This is virtually a no-fail recipe that makes a biscuit-style, slightly sweet cake. It is a perfect counterpoint to the luscious richness of ripe summer strawberries.

MAKES 6 TO 8 SERVINGS

1 cup self-rising flour
1 cup plus 1 pint heavy whipping cream
½ cup powdered sugar
1 quart ripe strawberries
Sugar to taste

• • • Preheat the oven to 400ºF. Stir together the flour, 1 cup of the whipping cream, and powdered sugar in a large bowl until a dough forms. Drop by 2 tablespoonsful on a greased baking sheet. Place in the center of the oven.

Bake 10 to 12 minutes or until golden brown. Split the cakes in half and cool.

Wash, hull, core, and drain the strawberries. Slice them lengthwise, reserving enough perfect whole berries to garnish each cake. Whip the remaining pint of whipping cream with sugar to taste. Place a large dollop of whipped cream on each cake; top with sliced berries and more whipped cream. Top with a whole berry.

—Ms. Dora Finley

. . . .

Strawberry Cake

Frozen strawberries bring the flavor of summer to you all year round. This is an easy and very attractive special-occasion cake. Make it for the Couples' Ministry on Valentine's Day.

MAKES 16 SERVINGS

1 (2-layer) package white cake mix
1 (3-ounce) package strawberry gelatin
4 large eggs
½ cup salad oil
½ cup thawed frozen strawberries, crushed
½ cup water
Frosting (recipe follows)

• • • Preheat the oven to 350ºF. Combine all the ingredients in a large bowl; beat 4 minutes. Pour into 2 greased and lightly floured 9-

inch cake pans. Bake for 35 minutes or until cake tests done. Remove cake from pans. Cool on a wire rack. Spread frosting between layers and on top.

NOTE: Serve topped with vanilla or strawberry ice cream and fresh strawberries. Cake can be made in two heart-shaped pans for Valentine's Day.

FROSTING
½ cup frozen crushed strawberries
¼ cup butter or margarine
1 (16-ounce) package powdered sugar

Combine all ingredients in a medium bowl; beat with electric mixer until smooth.

—*Mrs. Lucille Battle*

Blueberry Sour Cream Cake

When everyone in church expects you to bring the same old thing to the Cake Walk, try this recipe and set tongues to wagging about your versatility.

MAKES 8 SERVINGS

1½ cups all-purpose flour
1 cup sugar, divided
½ cup (1 stick) butter or margarine
1½ teaspoons baking powder
1 large egg
2 teaspoons vanilla, divided

1 quart fresh blueberries, washed and destemmed
2 cups sour cream
2 large egg yolks

• • • Preheat the oven to 350°F. Grease a 9-inch baking pan. Combine the flour, ½ cup of the sugar, butter, baking powder, 1 egg, and 1 teaspoon of the vanilla in a large bowl; mix thoroughly. Turn into the prepared pan and sprinkle evenly with the blueberries. Combine the sour cream, egg yolks, the remaining ½ cup sugar, and the remaining 1 teaspoon vanilla in a medium bowl; blend well. Pour over berries. Bake for 1 hour or until edges are lightly browned.

—*Mrs. Gracie Briggs*

Night-and-Day Marble Cake

Black-and-white, or marble, cake has gone by lots of names over the years. Someone brought this cake to the Black History Month potluck supper as a way to introduce a discussion of integration to the younger generation.

MAKES 12 TO 14 SERVINGS

2 cups sifted cake flour
2 teaspoons baking powder
¼ teaspoon salt
½ cup butter or margarine
1 cup sugar

2 large eggs, well beaten
⅔ cup milk
1 teaspoon ground cinnamon
½ teaspoon ground cloves
½ teaspoon ground nutmeg
2 tablespoons molasses
Butter Frosting (page 175)

• • • Preheat the oven to 350°F. Sift together the flour, baking powder, and salt three times in a large bowl; set aside. Cream the butter and sugar in a large bowl until light and fluffy. Add the eggs. Add the flour mixture, alternately with the milk. Beat after each addition until the mixture is smooth. Divide the batter into two parts. Add the cinnamon, cloves, nutmeg, and molasses to one part. Alternately drop tablespoons of dark batter and light batter into a greased 8-by-4-inch loaf pan. Bake for 1 hour or until done. Cool on a rack; remove from the pan. Spread Butter Frosting on top and sides of cake.

—*adapted from* The Southern Cookbook of Fine Old Recipes

Chocolate Chocolate Cupcakes

Children will love these cupcakes because of the super chocolate taste and parents will love you because while the powdered sugar makes a mess, it won't stain their little ones' Sunday clothes.

1½ cups all-purpose flour
½ cup sugar
¼ cup unsweetened cocoa powder
½ teaspoon baking soda
½ teaspoon salt
½ cup orange juice
⅓ cup water
3 tablespoons vegetable oil
1 tablespoon vinegar
1 teaspoon vanilla
⅓ cup semisweet chocolate mini-morsels
Powdered sugar

• • • Preheat the oven to 375°F. Place paper baking cups in 12 cups of a muffin pan. Combine the flour, sugar, cocoa powder, baking soda, and salt in one bowl. Combine the juice, water, oil, vinegar, and vanilla in another bowl. Mix the dry ingredients, liquid ingredients, and chocolate mini-morsels together just until blended. Spoon into baking cups, filling two-thirds full. Bake for 12 minutes. Remove from pans and sift powdered sugar over the cupcakes.

—*Joyce Fourth*

CHAPTER 2

Pies, Cobblers, and Turnovers

Mrs. Della Thurston, left, offers a Dixie cup of punch to Mrs. Lottie Twyner Rhodes at a church reception as Brenda Rhodes, center, looks on smiling. Tuskegee, AL, 1964.

Idle Hands Are the Devil's Tools

When my younger sister's pastor asked her to be a Communion Steward, she was undone, totally baffled, mortally offended, and as young people say these days, she was too through. She was devoted to her church and willingly served in many capacities, but she just didn't think she was Communion Steward material. Yet.

As far as my sister was concerned, the only women who could rightly be Communion Stewards were devout, pious, settled widow women or maiden ladies of a certain age, who served God by preparing Communion each first Sunday. She couldn't imagine herself in the job because she had young children and a living husband. Whoever heard of a Communion Steward dancing at Mardi Gras balls or wearing high-heeled shoes and nail polish? My sister considered herself both too young and too much of the world for the exalted position we had revered all our lives.

Our beloved grandmother, old when we were children, had been a Communion Steward at Samuel Chapel AME Zion Church in Prichard, Alabama. Lottie Twyner Rhodes was a stout, sturdy woman who wore sensible low-heeled, tie-up shoes that she labeled "old lady comforts."

With her steel gray eyes and matching bun, Grandmother was a formidable presence in our lives. When we were too young to go to school ourselves and too young to be left at home alone, we spent our days with Grandmother while our parents taught school. Grandmother dragged us along to all her church meetings, whether we wanted to go or not. Indeed, we never imagined then that we had a choice. If Grandmother had a meeting or an appointment, so did we.

The Communion Steward meetings rotated from house to house among the other old ladies who worked in the church with Grandmother. They might have been old, but they were sticklers for protocol, carrying both their Bibles and their copies of *Robert's Rules of Order* to every meeting.

Each meeting of the Communion Stewards opened with a prayer. Next, after much discussion among the assembled ladies, there was an agenda to approve, followed by an interminable business meeting that felt to us like it lasted for four hundred hours. Fidgeting was not an option. As children, we learned patience, playing quietly until the meeting was over. At the end, there was a meal crowned with dessert, often our grandmother's delicious sweet potato munge, a treat no one in our family remembers how to make.

Throughout each meeting of the Communion Stewards, as at any other rare moment when she sat still, Grandmother kept her hands busy with crochet. She made lace edging for altar cloths and pillowcases, pineapple-stitch-pattern coverlets and matching dust ruffles for every bed in her house, intricate crocheted tablecloths for each of her daughters, and scarves without number, which she taught us, her granddaughters, how to "do up." This doing up was an involved process by which clean, wet, crocheted scarves were dipped in boiled starch, laid flat on a towel, and shaped around empty Coca-Cola bottles to dry with the requisite ruffles.

With all her heart, Grandmother believed two things: that idle hands were the devil's tools (even when her own hands were gnarled with arthritis), and that cleanliness was next to godliness. There was always a whole lot of boiling, bleaching, and bluing going on in Grandmother's house, especially when it was time to prepare for Communion.

Grandmother and her fellow Communion Stewards took great pride in how their church looked. Each first Sunday, they dressed the Communion table with linens embroidered and crocheted by their own hands, then bleached and blued to blazing whiteness. They tied yards of dazzling white cloths to cover the altar rail. To us children, these coverings looked a lot like the dust ruffles that adorned all the beds in Grandmother's house.

More often than not, the flower arrangements that graced the altar also came from the gardens of the Communion Stewards. Whatever was in season was what they brought. Azaleas, hydrangeas, roses, bridal wreaths, mums—the Communion Stewards had flowers for every season.

Once a month, on the Saturday before Communion Sunday, we had a job to do. We took turns standing on a chair at the sink in Grandmother's kitchen to wash each and every teeny tiny little communion cup before Grandmother sterilized them in boiling water. Later, the stewards would prepare countless trays of these thimble-sized glass cups filled with Welch's grape juice. They arranged shining platters heaped high with broken, unsalted Uneeda biscuit crackers for the pastor and deacons to pass to all the members. And all too often, the number of people waiting to take communion exceeded the number of available communion cups

Dressed in their sensible low-heeled oxfords, neat white dresses, and jaunty black berets, the stewards would form a relay team, like volunteer firefighters. They collected trays of dirty, used cups and passed them to other stewards who rushed to the kitchen. There, yet a third group of waiting stewards dipped the cups in hot, soapy water and hotter rinse water. Still other stewards refilled the cups and dashed back to replenish the sanctuary with full trays of clean, filled cups in no time flat. Despite their best efforts, however, there was sometimes a lag in the service.

None of the Communion Stewards liked this system, but they made it work until Grandmother and her cohorts determined to put an end to their rushed first Sunday exercises. They vowed to raise the money to buy enough sufficient glass cups so they could sterilize and fill all the cups in advance and Communion could be served to the entire church at one time.

Every summer, my grandmother organized a "Country Fair" at her church. All the Communion Stewards sold aprons and patchwork pillows they made from scraps. They sold fig and peach preserves they'd put up with fruit from their gardens, and countless decorative items they had crocheted or embroidered. They offered dinners of fried fish or fried chicken, with sides of English peas, potato salad, a pear-half dressed with a blob of mayonnaise topped with a maraschino cherry, and homemade lemon pound cake for dessert. These dinners sold for $1.50 each.

Every year Grandmother pieced and quilted an elaborate patchwork bed cover, which she raffled off at her Country Fair. Some years it was a "crazy quilt" made of velvet scraps. Other years it was a Log Cabin pattern or a Wedding Ring quilt. She always priced the chances at four for a dollar and if you bought at least $5 worth of chances, you improved your possibility of winning the quilt. Nobody complained about gambling back then, at least not to Grandmother.

Each spring, Grandmother gave her granddaughters brown paper patterns, sharp scissors, pins, and piles of fabric scraps. She showed us how to cut out quilt pieces and sew them together by hand. Using her iron, which must have weighed fifty pounds, we learned how to press the seams flat. When we were older, she taught us how to lay the batting smooth and quilt the top and the backing together by hand, with stitches so fine they were almost invisible.

Her Country Fair raffle quilt was a different matter. It was always brightly colored and elaborate—slightly showy, even—so people would oooh and aaah when they saw it, buying up lots of chances in hopes of winning the prize. The Country Fair quilt was nothing like the sensible and serviceable ones she made for her family. And Grandmother stitched the whole thing together on her ancient Singer sewing machine in no time flat.

Grandmother and her sister Communion Stewards may have held their Country Fair to raise money to buy glass communion cups, but for us, it was a time to have fun being with the old ladies and learning from them.

Nowadays, many churches put Communion in disposable plastic cups. Use them once and throw them away. Some churches even serve Communion in prepackaged pop-top cups with the wafer and the grape juice in a single foil-wrapped container. Something tells me Grandmother and her Communion Stewards would not have approved of that innovation.

Rich Pie Dough

When there's no fresh fruit on hand because everything is out of season, use this rich dough for your piecrust. It can elevate even canned fruit to heights of taste greatness.

MAKES 2 (9-INCH) PIECRUSTS

2 cups all-purpose flour
¼ teaspoon salt
2 tablespoons powdered sugar
⅔ cup shortening
⅛ cup cold butter or margarine
5 tablespoons cold water

• • • Sift the flour, salt, and sugar together in a large bowl. Cut in the shortening and butter. Add cold water by tablespoonsful until the dough binds. Turn the dough onto floured waxed paper. Knead lightly to combine all ingredients. Roll away from you until about ¼

inch thick. Line 2 (9-inch) pie plates. Bake according to pie recipe you are using.

—*adapted from* **Rumford Complete Cookbook**

Less-Fat Piecrust

If you're watching your waistline and counting your calories, you've probably already given up pie, but that's no reason to stop baking for your family and friends. Here's a recipe with less fat.

MAKES 3 (9-INCH) DOUBLE PIECRUSTS

3 cups all-purpose flour
1 cup melted shortening
1 cup cold water
Pinch of salt

• • • Combine all ingredients in a medium bowl. Work the dough with your hands. Add extra water, if needed, to make dough stiff enough to roll out. Roll dough to about ⅛-inch thickness. Line pie plates. Flute edges. Bake as directed in specific pie recipe.

—*adapted from* **Rumford Complete Cookbook**

. . . .

Cake Crumb Crust

This recipe is a good example of putting the maxim "Waste not, want not" into action. Plus, stale cake crumbs make a wonderfully textured crust that tastes really good.

MAKES 1 (9-INCH) PIECRUST

3 cups stale cake cubes (pound cake or cake without frosting works best)

• • • Preheat the oven to 350°F. Crumble the cake into crumbs. Pat the crumbs into the bottom and up the sides of a 9-inch pie pan. Put another pie pan on top of the crumbs and press down to shape the crumbs into the bottom pie plate. Bake 10 to 15 minutes. Cool before filling. This crust works well with ice-cream pies.

—*Mrs. Beulah Hughes*

. . . .

Dough Dough

You should certainly use Dough Dough as the crust in your favorite cobbler recipe. No matter how good your cobbler is now, this will make it even better. It is so good, you could even forget about the filling. Bake a batch of dough, sprinkle it with sugar, and eat it all by itself.

MAKES ENOUGH DOUGH FOR
TWO (9 INCH) CRUSTS

3 to 3½ cups self-rising flour
½ pound butter, softened
4 large egg yolks
½ to ¾ cup sugar
2 teaspoons milk or sour cream
Dash of vanilla
Zest of 1 lemon
3–4 tablespoons ice water

• • • Combine all the ingredients in a large bowl. Add ice water as needed to help dough bind together. Work together with your hands to form a smooth ball of dough. Divide the dough into two parts. Chill for 30 minutes.

Preheat the oven to 375°F. Roll out each part of dough with a rolling pin to about ⅛ inch thick. Use one to line the bottom and up the sides of a baking dish. Prick the dough with a fork. Bake in the oven for 5 to 7 minutes or until lightly browned. Remove from the oven. Add the filling of your choice. Place second rolled-out dough on the top of the fill-ing. Pinch edges. Bake for 30 minutes or until done.

NOTE: For a tasty snack, roll out both parts of the dough, lay on cookie sheets, and bake at 400°F. Cut or break into pieces. Enjoy!

—*Ms. Zoë Marie Isaac Gadsen*

. . . .

Peach Cobbler

Use really ripe peaches or even a mix of ripe peaches and ripe nectarines for this cobbler. An after "Meeting" dinner without a peach cobbler is like Sunday service without singing.

MAKES 6 TO 8 SERVINGS

1 cup sugar
¾ cup milk
½ cup all-purpose flour
1 teaspoon vanilla
2 teaspoons baking powder
Dash of salt
2 tablespoons shortening
3 cups sliced peaches
Dough Dough (see recipe page 55), unbaked

• • • Preheat the oven to 375°F. Combine all the ingredients in a large bowl, mixing well. Prepare Dough Dough. Follow the directions to complete the cobbler. Serve warm.

—*Mrs. Mirtie Smith*

. . . .

Fruit Crumb Pie

At the end of a week-long Revival, there's nothing better than this pie to keep spirits high.

MAKES 1 (9-INCH) PIE

⅓ cup all-purpose flour
⅓ cup oatmeal
¼ cup packed dark brown sugar
⅛ teaspoon baking soda
Pinch of salt
⅓ teaspoon cinnamon
¼ cup melted butter or margarine
1 (20-ounce) can blueberry or
* cherry pie filling*
1 (9-inch) unbaked piecrust

• • • Preheat the oven to 425°F. Combine the flour, oatmeal, brown sugar, baking soda, salt, and cinnamon in a small bowl. Add the melted butter and mix thoroughly until all the ingredients are moistened; set aside. Spoon the pie filling into the unbaked piecrust. Add the crumb mixture over the top. Bake for 25 to 30 minutes, or until the filling bubbles and the crumb mixture browns.

—*Mrs. Lucille Battle*

. . . .

The Church Ladies' Divine Desserts

Gritty Pie

MS. MIRTIE SMITH

College Hill Presbyterian Church
Dayton, Ohio

These days, when folks want to make a fruit cobbler or a pie, they open up a can or head for the produce department. But it wasn't always that easy, as Mirtie Smith can tell you. "I made my first blackberry pie when I was nine years old, with berries I hand-picked myself. My mother was out of town," says the Tennessee native, who now lives in Trotwood, Ohio. "I wanted to have something nice for her when she got home."

"It wasn't my best pie. I didn't wash the blackberries as thoroughly as I needed to, and the results were disastrous. No one wanted to eat that gritty pie," she remembers with a laugh. "But they did.

"My mother, touched by the gesture, silenced the unfavorable reviews of my siblings with a curt, 'Eat it!'"

People have been eating Mirtie Smith's cooking gladly ever since; but today, they give it rave reviews. Her pastor, Rev. Robert Jones of College Hill Presbyterian Church, can't say enough good things about her cooking, and his enjoyment is obvious.

Mirtie Smith has been a member of College Hill for nearly thirty years, and she's still making pies. She cooks for all sorts of church events—funerals, potluck dinners, the church's "bodacious meat-loaf dinner," and special occasions such as when visitors come to dine at the church. On those days, the women of College Hill break out the linen tablecloths to serve their guests in style.

Mirtie Smith enjoys cooking because it is so relaxing, and it's a way to serve that gives her great pleasure. When she's not in the church kitchen helping to feed others, she is in a church pew getting fed spiritually. She loves the quiet dignity of her church and the way her pastor teaches as well as preaches.

"When I come away, I'm feeling good," she says.

Cherry Glazed Pie

Come February, churches celebrate Black History Month and an occasional mention of Washington cutting down his cherry tree. This recipe is a good way to remember both.

MAKES 6 TO 8 SERVINGS

1 cup sweetened condensed milk
⅓ cup lemon juice
1 teaspoon vanilla
½ teaspoon almond extract
½ cup whipping cream, whipped
½ cup slivered almonds
1 (9-inch) graham cracker crust
1 (16-ounce) can pitted tart cherries
¼ cup sugar
1 teaspoon cornstarch
Red food coloring

• • • Combine the milk, lemon juice, vanilla, and almond extract in a medium bowl; mix well. Fold in the whipped cream and almonds. Spoon into the graham cracker crust. Drain the cherries, reserving ⅔ cup juice. Combine the juice, sugar, and cornstarch in a medium saucepan over medium heat. Cook, stirring constantly, until thick and clear. Remove from the heat. Stir in the drained cherries and a few drops of food coloring. Let cool. Spoon over the pie. Chill until ready to serve.

Apple Dumplings

Good hot or cold, Apple Dumplings can make you shout.

MAKES 6 SERVINGS

2 cups all-purpose flour
4 teaspoons baking powder
1 teaspoon salt
4 tablespoons shortening
1 cup milk
6 medium Rome apples, pared and cored
6 tablespoons sugar
3 tablespoons cinnamon

• • • Preheat the oven to 350°F. Sift together the flour, baking powder, and salt in a large bowl. Cut in the shortening. Add the milk and mix well until the dough is smooth. Turn onto a floured board and divide the dough into 6 portions. Roll each portion large enough to cover 1 apple. Center an apple on each piece of dough. Combine the sugar and cinnamon. Fill the center of each apple with the sugar/cinnamon mixture. Wet edges of the dough. Fold up over the apple and pinch edges together. Place on a greased baking sheet, and bake for 30 minutes or until the apples are tender.

—*adapted from* Edith Barber's Cookbook

Talking the Talk and Walking the Walk

MISS JOYCE ANN FOURTH
Mount Joy Baptist Church
Washington, D.C.

Miss Joyce Ann Fourth was a child of the seventies who used to drive a bright orange 1974 Volkswagen Beetle. Her sporty little bug, bearing the vanity license plates "4 TH-E," announced her nickname as it ferried her about for many years until it finally bit the dust, breaking her heart in the process. Whether wearing her white usher's uniform for Sunday service, her tailored suede bermuda shorts and silk blouses to scholarship meetings, or her colorful African-inspired dresses to afternoon programs, Fourthy now goes to church in a more sedate vehicle.

Never one to wear her faith on her sleeve, no matter how she is dressed, Fourthy is a deeply religious woman who demonstrates her kindness to young and old alike on a daily basis. Not only does she visit the sick and shut-in; she also takes food and does chores for friends and church members who are unable to care for themselves—not once in a while, but on a regular and consistent basis.

She grew up in her church and was a member of the Senior Usher Board for nine years. As chair of her church's Scholarship Committee for nearly four years, she took the lead in raising thousands of dollars to help fund college educations for young church members.

But her dedication to helping young people doesn't mean she's soft on slackers. Miss Joyce, as the children of the church all call her—never daring to use her nickname—is known far and wide for her pithy sayings as well as her kind heart. She once declared that a scholarship applicant who failed to complete the necessary paperwork was "so lazy he wouldn't take a job in a pie factory eating crust."

Her true ministry is helping children to succeed. She takes a special interest in teenagers who are having trouble in school, encouraging them to keep trying, helping them with their homework, and insisting that they read, read, and read some more. Miss Fourth always seems to know where a teen can find a summer job, and has been known to visit the work site to make sure everything was going well.

A stately, dignified church lady with warm brown eyes and a wicked sense of humor, Fourthy turns into a child herself when the circus comes to town. Not wanting to look foolish about her enthusiasm for elephants, clowns, and those daring young men on the flying trapeze, she always takes two or three children with her when she makes her annual pilgrimage to the big top. Next year, she pledges to make it to the circus parade and maybe even take a ride on one of those elephants—with or without her young charges in tow.

You can bet she'll find a way to get complimentary tickets for the children. She is so persuasive she could, in her own words, "beg a wild coon tame."

Apple Fritters

These fritters are so light you can eat as many as you like. Serve them to the Youth Group after a community service project.

MAKES 6 TO 8 SERVINGS

2 cups all-purpose flour
2 large egg yolks
1 teaspoon brandy
½ teaspoon salt
1 cup milk
2 large egg whites
4 large cooking apples
Oil for frying (about 1 cup)
½ cup powdered sugar

• • • Place the flour in a large bowl and make a well in the center. Add the egg yolks, the brandy, and the salt in the well and work into the flour until it is thoroughly mixed. Add the milk gradually until the batter is smooth. Beat the egg whites in a medium bowl until stiff. Fold into the batter. Peel and core the apples. Cut the apples into ⅛-inch rounds. Dip each apple piece in the batter. Heat the oil in a large frying pan or an electric frying pan (about 375°F.). Fry the battered apple pieces in the hot oil, turning until crispy on all sides. Drain on paper towels. Sprinkle with the powdered sugar while warm and serve immediately.

—adapted from **Tante Marie's French Kitchen**

Apple Pie

"Flavorful with natural juices, this apple pie tastes just like my grandma's prize-winning Sunday supper dessert recipe," admits our kitchen tester.

MAKES 1 (9-INCH) PIE (8 SLICES)

Enough pie dough for one double-crust
    9-inch pie (page 54)
All-purpose flour to dust surface
1 large egg white, lightly beaten
1 teaspoon cinnamon
1½ tablespoon cornstarch
¾ cup sugar
Pinch of nutmeg
1 tablespoon lemon juice
5 cups peeled, cored, sliced cooking apples
1 to 2 tablespoons unsalted butter, cut in
    small pieces

• • • Preheat the oven to 450°F. Roll half of the pie dough on a lightly floured surface to fit a 9-inch pie plate. Shape the dough into the plate, leaving about a 1-inch overhang. Brush the dough with half of the egg white to keep it from getting soggy when the apples are added. Combine the cinnamon, cornstarch, sugar, nutmeg, and lemon juice in a large bowl. Add the apples and toss gently. Place the coated apples in the piecrust. Dot with pieces of butter. Roll out the remaining pie dough. Moisten the rim of the bottom crust with water. Cover with the top crust, trimming any excess. Press the crusts together lightly around the rim, turn them under, and crimp decoratively. Cut six 2-inch slits evenly around the top of the pie for steam to escape and to test apples for doneness after baking. Brush the crust with the remaining egg white to glaze. Place the pie on the center rack of the oven. Reduce the temperature to 350°F, and bake for 1 hour. Cool on a pie rack. Serve slightly warm or at room temperature. Top each slice with a scoop of ice cream or a slice of Cheddar cheese if you desire.

—Family and Friends Favorite Recipes

Bourbon Apple Pie

No matter how you slice it, this bourbon-enhanced apple pie is a crowd pleaser. Even for teetotalers.

MAKES 8 SERVINGS

¾ cup raisins

2–3 tablespoons bourbon

Pastry (recipe follows)

6–8 apples (a mix of tart and sweet),
    pared and thinly sliced

1 cup packed dark brown sugar

¼ cup butter or margarine, softened

2 tablespoons lemon juice

2 tablespoons all-purpose flour

½ cup sugar

¾ teaspoon cinnamon

¾ teaspoon nutmeg

¼ teaspoon salt

1 teaspoon grated lemon peel

2 tablespoons butter, melted

• • • Plump the raisins in the bourbon in a small bowl for several hours or heat and let sit for ½ hour; drain and set aside. Preheat the oven to 450°F. Make the pastry and roll out one crust. Place the pastry in a 9- or 10-inch pie plate as the bottom crust. Combine the raisins with the apples, brown sugar, ¼ cup butter, lemon juice, flour, sugar, cinnamon, nutmeg, salt, and lemon peel in a large bowl; mix well. Spoon into the piecrust. Drizzle the 2 tablespoons butter over the filling. Roll out the remaining pastry and place on top of pie, crimping edges together. Prick top with a fork and bake for 10 minutes; reduce the temperature to 350°F. and bake 40 minutes.

PASTRY

3 cups all-purpose flour

4 tablespoons powdered sugar

1 teaspoon salt

⅔ cup shortening

2 large egg yolks

8 tablespoons ice water (may need more)

Sift together the flour, sugar, and salt in a medium bowl. Cut in the shortening. Blend the yolks and water together in a small bowl. Gradually add to the flour mixture, adding more water if needed. Chill the dough while assembling the filling. Roll dough to ⅛-inch thickness.

—Mrs. Doris Hicks

Apple Turnovers

These pastries are excellent the second day and pack well for church picnics or in a Vacation Bible School lunch box.

MAKES 5 SERVINGS

CRUST

2 cups all-purpose flour

1 teaspoon salt

1 teaspoon ground nutmeg

1 teaspoon ground cinnamon

1 teaspoon ground allspice

⅔ cup shortening

⅛ cup cold butter or margarine

6–7 tablespoons water

• • • Sift dry ingredients together. Cut in butter and shortening. Add 6 to 7 tablespoons of water so the dough holds together. Gently knead the dough. Turn onto floured board and roll to about ⅜ inch thick. Cut into 5-inch squares.

FILLING

2 cups firm, tart apples, peeled, cored, chopped

1 cup sugar

1 teaspoon cinnamon or apple pie spice

Preheat the oven to 450°F. Combine the apples, sugar, and cinnamon in a medium bowl. Place 3 to 4 tablespoons filling on each square. Fold into triangles. Wet inside edges with a small amount of water. Press edges together and seal with a fork dipped into water. Make three slashes in each turnover so steam can escape. Place turnovers about 2 inches apart on a greased cookie sheet. Bake 15 minutes. Reduce heat to 350°F and bake 15 minutes longer.

NOTE: You can frost or glaze the turnovers if you want a really sweet treat.

—Mrs. Carolyn L. Rhodes

• •

Butterscotch Pie

A beautiful meringue-topped pie, this recipe is a favorite make-ahead dessert for church suppers.

MAKES 1 (9-INCH) PIE

1 cup brown sugar

1 tablespoon butter

1 large egg, separated

2 tablespoons all-purpose flour

1 cup milk

1 teaspoon vanilla

1 (9-inch) piecrust, baked

1 large egg white

1 teaspoon sugar

• • • Preheat the oven to 400°F. Combine the brown sugar, butter, egg yolk, and flour in a medium saucepan. Stir in the milk; mix well.

Place the saucepan over medium heat and cook mixture until thick, stirring constantly. Stir in the vanilla. Pour into the baked pie-crust. Beat the egg white and the 1 teaspoon sugar in a medium bowl until stiff. Spoon over the pie filling. Bake the pie just until the egg white browns. Cool and refrigerate before serving.

—*adapted from* The Southern Cookbook of Fine Old Recipes

Baptism by Fire

MISS MAYBELLE POLK
Pilgrim Rest Baptist Church
El Campo, Texas

Miss Maybelle Polk joined Pilgrim Rest Baptist Church when she was seven years old and she continued as a faithful member of the church for more than sixty-seven years, until her death in 1998. Although her church was built on the banks of a river, the only time the water rose high enough for baptism by immersion was when the river reached flood stage, which happened only three or four times a year—not a regular-enough event to allow for monthly baptism.

To solve this problem, the church decided to dig a wide, deep excavation for its baptisms. El Campo is a low-lying town, just twelve miles from the Gulf of Mexico, so any hole quickly fills up with groundwater. But in addition to filling up with water, this hole also filled up with snakes, mostly water moccasins.

When it came time for the child Miss Maybelle Polk to be baptized, and indeed before each monthly baptism service, the deacons gathered at the excavation. Armed with their .22 rifles, they cleared out the snakes so the pastor and candidates for baptism might safely enter the water. Since a snake was responsible for Eve's fall from grace, no one objected to the monthly slaughter. Then, during the service, a few deacons stood armed and ready to shoot any snake that might rear its ugly head.

This tradition ended in 1944 when Pilgrim Rest installed its indoor pool for baptism.

Pumpkin Pie

The Harvest Festival would not be complete without several versions of pumpkin pie. This recipe is a spicy and delicious way to use the abundance of fall pumpkins.

MAKES 6 TO 8 SERVINGS

2 cups cooked pumpkin

1 cup sugar

½ teaspoon salt

1 teaspoon cinnamon

1 teaspoon ginger

¼ teaspoon ground cloves
   (optional)

1 pint scalded milk

2 large eggs, well beaten

1 (9-inch) deep-dish piecrust

• • • Preheat the oven to 350°F. Combine the pumpkin, sugar, salt, cinnamon, ginger, ground cloves (if desired), milk, and eggs in a large bowl; mix well. Pour the mixture into the piecrust. Bake for 50 minutes or until the pie tests done.

—Mrs. Willette Bailey

In 1979 Mrs. Carol Preston and four other volunteers created the "Pacesetters," a weekly program of Christian education, Bible study, arts and crafts, music and enrichment activities for children ages 3–12. More than a thousand children have benefited from this innovative Children's Ministry.

Pudding Pie

If you have to make a last-minute pie for a funeral repast, this recipe calls for ingredients you're likely to have on hand. That in no way minimizes how good it tastes.

MAKES 8 SERVINGS

¾ cup granulated sugar
¾ cup packed dark brown sugar
½ cup whipping cream
2 large eggs, separated
2 tablespoons butter or margarine
½ teaspoon vanilla
Nutmeg to taste
1 (9-inch) piecrust, unbaked

• • • Preheat the oven to 275°F. Combine the sugars, cream, egg yolks, and butter in the top of a double boiler. Cook, stirring often, until mixture is thickened. Remove the pan from the heat. Stir in the vanilla. Beat the egg whites until stiff peaks form; fold into the batter. Pour the mixture into the piecrust. Sprinkle with nutmeg. Bake 1 to 1¼ hours or until the custard is set. Remove from oven, cool on a wire rack, and then refrigerate. Serve cold with ready-made whipped topping sprinkled with nutmeg, if desired.

—Mrs. Carol Preston

Spirited Pecan Pie

All the alcohol in the rum cooks out, but the delicious tropical flavor remains.

MAKES 6 TO 8 SERVINGS

½ cup butter or margarine, softened
½ cup sugar
1 cup light corn syrup or Alaga (a corn/cane syrup blend)
3 large eggs, lightly beaten
2 tablespoons rum
1 cup chopped pecans
Spirited Pastry (recipe follows)
¾ cup pecan halves

• • • Preheat the oven to 350°F. Cream the butter and sugar in a large bowl until light and fluffy. Add the corn syrup, eggs, and rum; beat well. Stir in the chopped pecans. Line a 9-inch pie pan with Spirited Pastry. Pour the filling into pastry, and top with pecan halves. Bake 55 minutes.

SPIRITED PASTRY

1 cup all-purpose flour
¼ teaspoon salt
6 tablespoons cold butter or margarine
2 to 3 tablespoons rum

Combine the flour and salt in a medium bowl; cut in the butter until the mixture resembles coarse meal. Sprinkle the rum over mixture, and stir until particles adhere when pressed gently. Shape dough into a ball, and chill 10 minutes before rolling out. Line a 9-inch pie shell.

—Mrs. Melanie Shelwood

Pudding Pecan Pie

There are as many good pecan pies as there are good cooks in a church. Fans of old-fashioned southern pecan pie will be pleasantly surprised with the puddinglike texture of this pie.

MAKES 6 TO 8 SERVINGS

1 (3¼-ounce) package vanilla or
    butterscotch pudding mix
1 cup dark corn syrup
¾ cup evaporated milk
1 large egg, slightly beaten
1½ cups chopped pecans
1 unbaked (9-inch) piecrust

• • • Preheat the oven to 350°F. Blend the pudding mix and the corn syrup in a large bowl. Gradually add the evaporated milk and the egg, stirring to blend. Stir in the pecans. Pour the mixture into the piecrust. Cover the rim of the piecrust with foil. Bake the pie for 35 to 40 minutes or until firm. Serve with ice cream or whipped cream, if desired.

—Mrs. Alice Butler

Sweet Potato Pecan Pie

Talk about gilding the lily! This recipe combines two old favorites into a tasty treat that can be served with pride from Thanksgiving through Christmas.

MAKES 6 TO 8 SERVINGS

1 pound sweet potatoes or yams, cooked
    and peeled
¼ cup butter or margarine
2 large eggs, lightly beaten
1 (14-ounce) can sweetened condensed milk
1 teaspoon grated orange rind
1 teaspoon vanilla extract
¼ teaspoon salt
1 teaspoon ground cinnamon
½ teaspoon ground nutmeg
1 (9-inch) unbaked piecrust
Pecan Topping (recipe follows)

• • • Preheat the oven to 350°F. Beat the hot yams with the butter in a large bowl. Add the eggs, milk, orange rind, vanilla extract, salt, cinnamon, and nutmeg. Mix well but don't overmix or the filling will resemble a soufflé. Pour into the piecrust. Bake for 50 minutes. Remove the pie from the oven and spoon the Pecan Topping evenly over the top. Bake for 20 to 25 minutes longer or until golden brown. Cool on a wire rack. Serve warm or chilled. Refrigerate the leftovers.

PECAN TOPPING

If you like pecans, you'll want this topping for all your autumn desserts.

1 large egg
3 tablespoons dark corn syrup
3 tablespoons light brown sugar
1 tablespoon butter or margarine, melted
½ teaspoon maple flavoring
½ cup chopped pecans

Combine the egg, corn syrup, sugar, butter, and maple flavoring in a medium bowl; mix well. Stir in the chopped pecans.

—Family and Friends Favorite Recipes

Aunt Emma's White Potato Pie

The story goes that when she discovered she didn't have a sweet potato in the house, Miss Emma just improvised and used white potatoes instead. That evening, she took the pie to church with her head held high.

MAKES 9 SERVINGS

2 large white potatoes
¼ pound butter or margarine
¾ cup sugar
2 large eggs, beaten
½ cup milk
1 teaspoon vanilla extract

½ teaspoon lemon extract
1 teaspoon or more allspice
1 (9-inch) piecrust

• • • Wash, then boil the potatoes in their skins in a saucepan until very soft. Let cool slightly, then peel. Preheat the oven to 350°F. Mash the potatoes with the butter in a large bowl using an electric mixer. Add the sugar, eggs, and milk. Add the seasonings; mix thoroughly. Pour into a 9-inch piecrust. Bake 40 minutes or until the pie begins to crack on top. Serve in small pieces topped with whipped cream if desired.

—Ms. Daisy A. Voigt

Lemon Meringue Pie

If your oven is hot as the fires of hell, be careful when making meringue. Often, a meringue will fail when the oven is too hot because the egg whites brown before they have time to set all the way through.

MAKES 6 TO 8 SERVINGS

1 cup plus 3 tablespoons water, divided
1 cup plus 2 tablespoons sugar, divided
3 tablespoons cornstarch
2 large eggs, separated
Juice of 1 lemon
Grated zest of 1 lemon
Pinch of salt
1 (8-inch) piecrust, baked

Two Halves of a Whole

MISS JULIA MAE STURKEY AND MISS WILLA MAE STURKEY
St. Luke AME Church
Opelika, Alabama

Janeula Burt, Ph.D., lives a long way from her relatives in Opelika, Alabama, but she never tires of talking about her twin cousins who are very special members of her family. Her favorite relatives have always been Miss Willa Mae and Miss Julia Mae Sturkey, the ones Jan looked forward to seeing whenever she went down South to visit.

Julia Mae and Willa Mae Sturkey were twin girls born in the early part of the century, around 1912. They lived all their lives in Opelika, Alabama. Janeula Burt can't untangle exactly how they are related to her, but she is pretty sure they are her cousins. They were contemporaries of her grandmother and of all her great-aunts, great-uncles, and older cousins. Like everyone in her family, they grew up and grew old in the Saint Luke African Methodist Episcopal Church, and, like so many twins, Julia and "Willie" were inseparable. Whenever you saw Julia, you knew Willie was somewhere very close by.

The misses Willa Mae and Julia Mae Sturkey, identical twin sisters, share a smile after Sunday school at St. Luke AME church. Their family has belonged to this church for over a hundred years.

Every day of their lives, they dressed alike. They looked so much alike, you'd have to really concentrate before you could tell who was who. Janeula Burt could usually tell them apart because, inevitably, Willie would smile and wink at her. Dr. Burt thinks Julia was born first, because, like a true older sister, she always looked after and took care of Willie. "Julia was usually very rigid and stern, but still very loving. Willie, on the other hand, was always full of hugs and kisses. If Willie wasn't close enough to acknowledge you, she would wait until your eyes met hers and she'd give you a smile and a wink, as though she knew a good joke she wanted to tell you later. Despite their personality differences, Julia and Willie complemented each other," explains Janeula Burt.

St. Luke was the center of their lives. Neither one of them ever learned to drive, so they walked everywhere they went, including to church, which was about two miles from their house. Both served on the Usher Board and both taught Sunday school. As they grew older, they became an integral part of the monthly Church Matrons board.

Even after they retired from doing domestic work, Julia and Willie kept active by working in their flower and vegetable gardens. They grew beautiful flowers and raised all kinds of vegetables. "Whenever we went to visit, there was always food cooking and it smelled so good you could hardly wait to sit down at the table. There was no such thing as a "light" meal at their house. Like most southern cooks, they prepared pork roasts, fried chicken, turnip greens, and always made big pitchers of southern "sweet tea," recalls Janeula Burt.

Willie passed away right before the last Christmas of the millennium, leaving Julia with no one to look after. "I am certain that for now, Willa Mae is the one looking after her big sister," says Janeula. "Maybe the reason for that knowing smile she always gave was that she knew no matter what, she and Julia would always be two halves of a whole."

• • • Preheat the oven to 300°F. Combine 1 cup of water and 1 cup of sugar in a medium saucepan. Boil the mixture until the sugar dissolves. Moisten the cornstarch with the 3 tablespoons of cold water. Stir the cornstarch into the saucepan; cook over medium heat for 5 minutes or until thickened. Combine the egg yolks, lemon juice, grated zest, and salt in a medium bowl. Add to the hot mixture, a little at a time, stirring after each addition. Cook over medium heat, stirring constantly, for 4 minutes or until very thick. Pour into the baked piecrust. Beat the egg whites in a medium bowl while slowly adding the remaining 2 tablespoons sugar; beat until the whites are stiff. Pile on the top of the pie, spreading to cover the lemon mixture completely. Bake about 10 minutes or until the egg whites are browned. Remove from the oven; place on a pie rack to cool and set for 1 hour. Refrigerate until ready to serve.

—Anyone Can Bake Cookbook

. . . .

Lemonade Pie

What would summer be without lemonade? And what would a church picnic be without this cool and refreshing pie?

MAKES 6 TO 8 SERVINGS

1 (8-ounce) can sweetened condensed milk

1 (6-ounce) can frozen lemonade, thawed

1 (4.5-ounce) container frozen whipped
    topping, thawed

1 (9-ounce) piecrust, baked

Whipped cream (optional)

• • • Combine the milk and lemonade in a medium bowl. Fold in the whipped topping. Spoon into the baked piecrust. Chill until ready to serve. Top with whipped cream, if desired.

—Mary Ellen Robinson

. . . .

Fresh Lime Pie

No one will blame you if you fail to confess that fresh squeezed limes are the secret to this elegant pie. If you like key lime pie, you'll love this one.

MAKES 8 SERVINGS

1 (9-inch) prepared graham cracker piecrust
    or Cookie Crust (recipe follows)

1 (12-ounce) can sweetened condensed milk

1 teaspoon lemon extract

3 large egg yolks

½ cup fresh squeezed lime juice

4 tablespoons fresh squeezed lemon juice

• • • Use prepared graham cracker piecrust or prepare Cookie Crust, if desired. Preheat the

oven to 350°F. Combine the milk, lemon extract, and egg yolks in a medium bowl. Beat well and slowly add the lime juice and the lemon juice. Pour into your prepared and cooled pie shell. Bake 15 minutes. Let it cool and settle into firmness before you refrigerate. Serve thoroughly chilled.

COOKIE CRUST

1½ cups chocolate wafer cookies

½ stick butter or margarine, melted

Preheat the oven to 375°F. Put the cookies in a zip-top bag; press out all the air and seal. Crush the cookies with a rolling pin or use your food processor or blender to pulse the cookies into 1½ cup crumbs. Combine the crumbs and butter in a medium bowl; press evenly into the bottom and up the sides of a 9-inch pie pan. Smooth the sides and bottom. Brown in the oven 15 minutes. Cool before filling.

—Ms. Brenda Rhodes Miller

. . . .

Lime Dream Pie

Church homecomings call for lots of desserts, but who wants to heat up the house in the summertime by turning on the oven? This easy and delicious pie is made on top of the stove . . . no sweat!

MAKES 6 TO 8 SERVINGS

1¼ cup sugar

½ cup sifted all-purpose flour

¼ teaspoon salt

1¾ cup water

1 (6-ounce) can frozen limeade, thawed

3 large egg yolks, slightly beaten

3 tablespoons butter

Cookie Crust (page 70)

Whipped cream (optional)

• • • Combine the sugar, flour, salt, water, and limeade in a medium saucepan. Cook over medium heat, stirring constantly, until the mixture thickens and boils. Then cook 2 minutes longer. Add a small amount of hot mixture to egg yolks. Add yolks to hot mixture; bring to a boil. Stir in the butter. Pour into the prepared Cookie Crust. Chill until ready to serve. Top with whipped cream, if desired.

—Mary Ellen Robinson

Frozen Margarita Pie

Whether you've taken the temperance pledge or not, you'll find Frozen Margarita Pie hard to resist.

MAKES 8 SERVINGS

1 (6-ounce) can frozen limeade

1 (8-ounce) can sweetened condensed milk

1 (8-ounce) container frozen whipped topping, thawed

1 teaspoon orange liqueur

1 (9-inch) graham cracker piecrust

• • • Combine the limeade, milk, whipped topping, and orange liqueur in a blender. Pour into piecrust. Freeze. Remove from freezer 20 minutes before serving.

—Mrs. Dora Finley

Raspberry Chiffon Pie

Fresh or frozen raspberries work equally well for this pie. Be sure to set aside some raspberries for garnish.

MAKES 6 TO 8 SERVINGS

4 cups raspberries

1 package gelatin

¼ cup cold water

1¼ cups sugar, divided

3 tablespoons lemon juice

½ teaspoon salt

4 large egg yolks, beaten

1 teaspoon grated orange rind

1 cup whipping cream

1 (9-inch) baked pie shell or
     chocolate cookie crust

• • • Set aside ¼ cup of the whole berries; mash the remainder and strain to remove seeds. Dissolve the gelatin in the cold water in a small bowl; let stand for 5 minutes. Combine the mashed berries, ¾ cup of the sugar, lemon juice, salt, and egg yolks in the top of a double boiler. Cook about 20 minutes or until thick, stirring frequently. Add the orange rind and dissolved gelatin. Stir thoroughly. Remove from the heat; cool. Beat the whipping cream with the remaining ½ cup sugar until soft peaks form. When raspberry mixture is cooled and thickened, fold in whipping cream. Pour into the baked pie shell and chill. Serve sliced and garnished with the reserved whole berries.

—*Brenda Rhodes Miller*

No Ways Tired

MRS. ALICE BUTLER
Mount Pisgah Church
Ridgeville, South Carolina

Mrs. Alice Butler has not let age or infirmity dampen her sense of humor one bit. "My husband is from Colmesmeil, Texas, a little bitty town that's near nothing in the middle of no where. That place is so small, by the time you call out the name, you're out of it. His mother was a member of Mount Zion Baptist Church, and she could cook! Oh my, she could cook. I use her buttermilk pie recipe to this day."

She speaks of her thirty-nine-year marriage and of her husband with real affection, "We are happy together because he is younger than I am, so he has enough energy to keep up with me. I'm not like a lot of old people you see who just like to sit around and wait to get older. I love to fish. We still go fishing every chance I get."

Mount Pisgah has been her church for about nine years. She used to sew and always donated fabric to the Senior Citizens Group at the church, but she has never joined it herself, though at seventy-five she is certainly entitled to be considered a senior citizen. When asked why she isn't a member of the group, Mrs. Butler replied, "I don't think it's fair to go to the group and eat those meals they make for old people who really need the food. We've been blessed, so I try to give more than I take."

Years ago, Mrs. Butler had a lyric soprano voice, but, she says, "I stopped singing and God took my talent away from me. I prayed and prayed to get my voice back. One day, all of a sudden, I could sing again, not like I used to, but I could sing. Praise the Lord."

Buttermilk Pie

Ask a Mother of the Church about this old-fashioned favorite that used ingredients on hand to make a lovely cream-colored pie.

MAKES 6 TO 8 SERVINGS

¼ cup all-purpose flour
Pinch of salt
1 cup sugar
1½ cups buttermilk
2 large eggs, slightly beaten
2 tablespoons butter or margarine, melted
1 teaspoon vanilla extract
1 unbaked (9-inch) deep-dish piecrust

• • • Preheat the oven to 350°F. Mix the flour, salt, and sugar in a large bowl. Add the buttermilk, eggs, butter, and vanilla. Stir to blend. Pour into the piecrust. Cover the piecrust rim with foil. Bake for about 35 minutes or until firm. Cool on a wire rack for 20 minutes. Cut and serve. Store unserved portion in the refrigerator.

—Mrs. Alice Butler, adapted from her mother-in-law's recipe

. . . .

Four-Layer Chocolate Pie

There's not a lot of cooking involved in making this four-layer treat, but true chocolate fans will thank you for bringing it to any church social.

MAKES 6 TO 8 SERVINGS

1 cup all-purpose flour
½ cup butter or margarine, melted
¾ cup finely chopped pecans, divided
1 (8-ounce) package cream cheese, softened
1 cup powdered sugar
4 cups frozen whipped topping, thawed
    and divided
1 (3-ounce) package instant chocolate
    pudding mix
1¾ cups milk
1 teaspoon vanilla
1 square Bakers semisweet chocolate, melted

• • • Preheat the oven to 350°F. Mix the flour, butter, and ½ cup of the pecans in a 9-inch pie plate and press into the plate to form the crust. Bake for 15 minutes. Cool.

Combine the cream cheese, powdered sugar, and 1 cup of the whipped topping in a medium bowl. Spread over the cooled crust. Combine the pudding mix, milk, and vanilla in a large bowl, mixing well. Spread over the cream cheese layer. Top the pie with the remaining 3 cups of whipped topping, drizzle with the melted chocolate, and garnish with the remaining ¼ cup chopped nuts. Chill for 1 hour before serving.

—Dr. Willie Creagh Bolden

. . . .

Fudge Pie

For those pie lovers who just like a hint of chocolate in a rich base, this pie is the perfect choice.

MAKES 6 TO 8 SERVINGS

¼ cup unsweetened cocoa powder
¼ cup all-purpose flour
1 cup sugar
1 stick butter or margarine, melted
2 large eggs, well beaten
2 teaspoons vanilla
1 (9-inch) pie shell, unbaked

• • • Preheat the oven to 350°F. Combine the cocoa powder, flour, and sugar in a large mixing bowl. Add the melted butter; mix well. Stir in the eggs and mix thoroughly. Stir in the vanilla, mix well. Pour mixture into the pie shell. Bake 30 minutes. Cool and serve with a dollop of whipped cream or softened vanilla ice cream.

—Ms. Melanie Shelwood

. . . .

Chess Pie

Make these tiny chess pies look like little jewels for your holiday bake sales. Center each in a square of brightly colored plastic wrap and tie with contrasting ribbons.

MAKES 14 SERVINGS

½ cup butter or margarine
1 cup sugar
3 large egg yolks
1 large egg white, stiffly beaten
1 cup chopped golden raisins
1 cup chopped pecans
1 teaspoon vanilla
14 individual-size prepared piecrusts
Whipped cream (optional)

• • • To make individual chess pies, use prepared piecrust from the dairy case. Cut squares slightly larger than the cups of a 12-cup muffin tin. Grease cups lightly and press dough into muffin cups.

Preheat the oven to 400°F. Cream the butter and sugar in a medium bowl. Add the egg yolks and egg white, stirring until foamy. Add the raisins and pecans; stir well. Pour into the piecrusts. Bake at 400°F for 15 minutes or until the filling is set; reduce the oven temperature to 350°F and bake about 10 minutes longer or until well browned. Serve with whipped cream if desired.

—adapted from The Southern Cookbook of Fine Old Recipes

. . . .

Chocolate Chess Pie

A Sunday school class can mix up the ingredients, bake the pie, and have it ready to serve after eleven-o'clock worship. It's that easy!

MAKES 6 TO 8 SERVINGS

1½ cups sugar
3½ tablespoons unsweetened cocoa powder
Pinch of salt
2 large eggs, beaten
¼ cup butter or margarine, melted
1 (6-ounce) can evaporated milk
1 teaspoon vanilla extract
1 (9-inch) unbaked piecrust

• • • Preheat the oven to 350°F. Combine the sugar, cocoa, and salt in a large bowl. Add the eggs, butter, milk, and vanilla; mix thoroughly. Pour into the piecrust. Bake for 45 to 50 minutes.

—Mary Ellen Robinson

Coconut Pie

Thank heaven even purists now allow the use of packaged coconut. In the old days, cracking a coconut and shredding the meat by hand was enough to make one lose her religion!

MAKES 6 TO 8 SERVINGS

3 large eggs, separated
½ cup sugar
Pinch of salt
2 cups scalded milk
½ cup shredded coconut
1 deep-dish pie crust

• • • Preheat the oven to 475°F. Beat the egg yolks with the sugar and salt in a large bowl. Beat the egg whites in a medium bowl until stiff peaks form. Fold into the egg yolk mixture. Stir in the milk, mixing well. Stir in the coconut. Pour into the piecrust (the filling will be piled high but will cook down). Place the pie on a baking sheet. Bake for 10 minutes. Reduce the oven temperature to 350°F and bake for 30 minutes longer.

—Mrs. Rita Stebbins

Coconut Custard Pie

Rich French custard and sweet coconut give this pie a wonderful taste of the Tropics.

MAKES 6 TO 8 SERVINGS

3 large eggs, well beaten
½ cup sugar
¼ teaspoon salt
2 cups cream
¾ cup shredded, sweetened coconut
1 teaspoon vanilla flavor
1 (9-inch) graham cracker piecrust

••• Preheat the oven to 450°F. Combine the eggs, sugar, salt, cream, coconut, and vanilla in a large bowl. Pour into the prepared 9-inch piecrust. Bake 15 minutes. Reduce the oven temperature to 325°F and bake 20 minutes longer or until the custard is set. Cool before slicing. Store unserved pie in the refrigerator.

—*Mrs. Carolyn L. Rhodes*

Fresh Strawberry Pie

When strawberries are in season, why not declare a Strawberry Sunday and bring this pie to celebrate the real taste of summer?

MAKES ONE (9-INCH) PIE

1 cup sugar
1 cup hot water
3 tablespoons cornstarch
3 tablespoons strawberry gelatin
2 cups strawberries, washed and sliced
1 (8-ounce) package cream cheese, softened
3 tablespoons powdered sugar
1 tablespoon milk
1 (9-inch) chocolate cookie crust (page 70)
Whipped cream for topping

••• Combine the sugar, hot water, and cornstarch in a medium saucepan. Bring to a boil. Stir until thickened. Remove from the heat. Stir in the strawberry gelatin. Let cool. Add the strawberries. Set mixture aside.

Mix the cream cheese, powdered sugar, and milk in a medium bowl. Spread on the chocolate cookie crust. Pour the strawberry mixture over the cream cheese. Refrigerate the pie for several hours or overnight. Serve topped with whipped cream.

NOTE: You can use a prepared graham cracker crust in place of the cookie crust.

—*Dr. Willie Creagh Bolden*

Banana Split Pie

This pie has enough jobs for several small helpers, and Sunday school children will enjoy both the making and the eating.

MAKES 6 SERVINGS

3 bananas, sliced
Lemon juice
1 (9-inch) graham cracker piecrust
1½ cups powdered sugar
1 (8-ounce) package cream cheese
1½ (8-ounce) cans crushed pineapple, drained
1 (8-ounce) container frozen whipped topping, thawed
½ cup chopped maraschino cherries
½ cup chopped peanuts or pecans (optional)

••• Moisten the sliced bananas with a small amount of lemon juice to prevent browning. Cover the graham cracker piecrust with the banana slices. Cream the sugar and cream cheese together in a medium bowl and spread over the bananas. Top the creamed mixture with the pineapple and then the whipped topping. Sprinkle with the cherries and nuts, if desired. Chill well before serving.

—Ms. Melanie Shelwood

. . . .

Pineapple Cream Pie

Several generations of church ladies in the author's family made this pie in the morning before going to Sunday school.

MAKES 6 SERVINGS

3 tablespoons cornstarch
1 tablespoon all-purpose flour
1 cup sugar
¼ teaspoon salt
1 teaspoon vanilla flavor
1 (16-ounce) can crushed pineapple
3 large eggs, separated
Sugar to taste
1 (9-inch) baked deep-dish piecrust

• • •Preheat the oven to 400°F. Sift together the cornstarch and flour in a large bowl; add the 1 cup sugar, salt, and vanilla. Drain the pineapple, pressing out all the juice and reserving it. Pour the dry ingredients into a heavy-bottom saucepan. Add all the juice slowly except for ¼ cup. Cook over medium heat, stirring until the mixture thickens. Beat the egg yolks in a small bowl; slowly add a little of the hot mixture to the egg yolks to warm them. Add the egg yolks slowly into the hot mixture, stirring constantly. Add 1 cup of the crushed pineapple, stirring until thick. Cool.

Combine the egg whites, the remaining ¼ cup pineapple juice, and sugar to taste in a medium bowl. Beat until stiff peaks form. Pour the cooled pineapple filling into the pie crust. Top with the egg white mixture. Bake until the meringue topping is brown. Cool before cutting.

—Mrs. Carolyn L. Rhodes

. . . .

Bethune Sweet Potato Pie

Mrs. Mary McLeod Bethune's sweet potato pies helped build the college that bears her name.

MAKES 3 PIES

9 medium sweet potatoes (about 4 pounds
*   or 6 cups mashed)*
¼ cup margarine, softened
½ cup granulated sugar
½ cup firmly packed light brown sugar
½ teaspoon salt
¼ teaspoon nutmeg
¼ teaspoon pumpkin pie spice
2 eggs, well beaten
2 egg whites
2 cups milk

1 tablespoon vanilla
3 unbaked (9-inch) standard piecrusts
Pecan or Walnut Topping (recipe follows)

• • • Boil the sweet potatoes in a large saucepan until fork tender. Peel and mash the potatoes.

Preheat the oven to 350°F. Combine the margarine, sugars, salt, nutmeg, and pumpkin pie spice in a large bowl. Beat at medium speed with an electric mixer until creamy. Beat in the sweet potatoes until well mixed. Beat in the eggs and egg whites. Slowly beat in the milk and the vanilla. Spoon the mixture into the unbaked pie shells, using about 3 cups filling per shell.

Bake for 50 to 60 minutes or until set. Cool to room temperature before serving. Serve the pie with whipped cream or Pecan or Walnut Topping. Refrigerate any leftover pie.

PECAN OR WALNUT TOPPING
¾ cup coarsely chopped pecans or walnuts
½ cup packed light brown sugar
3 tablespoons butter or margarine, melted

Mix the chopped nuts and the sugar in a small bowl. Add the melted butter; stir until moist. Sprinkle the mixture over cooled pie. Cover the crust edges with foil to avoid burning. Broil about 6 inches from the heat for 2 to 3 minutes or until bubbly. Cool before serving.

—*The* Black Family Dinner Quilt Cookbook *via* Dr. Dorothy I. Height

Blackberry Crunch

If you pick the blackberries yourself in the old churchyard, be sure to wash them well so they aren't gritty. For variety add half blackberries, half raspberries.

MAKES 6 TO 8 SERVINGS

1 pound fresh blackberries
2 tablespoons lemon juice
⅔ cup packed light brown sugar
½ cup all-purpose flour
⅔ cup quick-cooking rolled oats
5 tablespoons butter or margarine, softened
1 teaspoon cinnamon
Ice cream (optional)

• • • Preheat the oven to 375°F. Combine the berries and lemon juice in a medium bowl. Spread in the bottom of an 8-by-8-inch baking pan. Combine the sugar, flour, oats, butter, and cinnamon in a medium bowl; mix well. Sprinkle over berries. Bake for 30 minutes or until crisp. Serve warm. Top with ice cream, if desired.

—Ms. Beverly Crandall

All That Jazz

DR. LOUISE TAYLOR
Westminster Presbyterian Church
Washington, D.C.

With big dark eyes smiling beneath pixie bangs and a jaunty beret, Dr. Lou is the picture of cosmopolitan charm. She radiates warmth to Jazz Night old timers and newcomers alike.

Every Friday night her quiet Presbyterian church transforms itself into music central. Guests meet over a soul food dinner whose modest price is no indication of its quality. Fresh fish perfectly fried, spicy wings, black beans and rice, crunchy homemade cole slaw, bread pudding, and sweet potato pie are sure crowd pleasers. Not only does Dr. Lou keep the meal line moving, but she is also a driving force behind organizing the Jazz Nights that attract more than a hundred people each week.

Popular local and regional musicians, as well as national artists who might drop in for a set, make the Friday Jazz Nights at Westminster Presbyterian enormous hits. Originally the idea of one of the church's co-pastors, based on his ministry experiences in Detroit, the project really took wing with Dr. Lou's help.

"I've been involved with jazz for many years, hanging out with musicians, going to tapings and rehearsals. I knew a great many jazz musicians, so this was something that appealed to me immediately because it combined two things I loved, my faith and jazz," she explains.

Early on, Dr. Lou recruited musician friends to help launch Jazz Night. Word of mouth did the rest.

Dr. Louise Taylor runs the Delta Research and Education Foundation with the same calm grace she brings to her church work. Throughout her career, everything she's done has reflected her deep commitment to the Presbyterian Church.

"I'm from Jersey City, where I grew up Presbyterian. My parents were the only black members of the Lafayette Presbyterian Church. During college, I worked part-time for the church, developing programs for low-income families and their children in public housing. Later, when I did field work for NAACP, I was still very much involved in the Presbyterian Church.

"For me, the church is a very ordered and structured denomination, and I appreciate and welcome that. It keeps me focused on the fact that one must be the searcher, always trying to find the way to God," she states with her trademark smile.

If attendance at Jazz Night is any clue, an innovative music ministry is a powerful way to build many bridges as people seek their way to God. According to Dr. Lou, "People come for the music, the food, and the fellowship. It is a wondrous experience."

Miss Adelaide's Sweet Potato Cobbler

On the farm, sweet potatoes are stored in ricks which are pyramid-shaped mountains of straw and sweet potatoes. This recipe, a family specialty given to the contributor by her mother, Miss Adelaide, is a delicious way to use the abundance of sweet potatoes that are available in the fall.

MAKES 8 SERVINGS

FILLING

2 pounds sweet potatoes (about 6)
1 ¾ cups sugar
6-8 ounces butter or margarine
2 teaspoons cinnamon
1 teaspoon allspice
⅓ cup hot water
1 teaspoon vanilla flavoring
Pats of butter

• • • Prepare crust as directed below. Wrap dough in waxed paper and refrigerate 30 minutes or more to chill thoroughly. Boil the whole sweet potatoes in a large saucepan of water until done—about 30 minutes, or until tender; cool and remove skins.

Once the dough is chilled, divide it into two balls. Roll one ball to thickness of about ⅛ inch. Cut into squares and line a greased 1½-quart baking dish (dough should hang over pan sides about 1 inch or more).

Preheat the oven to 350°F. Cut each cooled and peeled sweet potato lengthwise into 3 or 4 slices. Layer half the potatoes on top of the dough in the prepared pan. Combine sugar, butter, cinnamon, and allspice in a medium bowl; mix well. Place half the mixture over the potatoes. Repeat layer of sweet potatoes and sugar mixture.

Roll out the remaining ball of dough to about ⅛ inch. Place on top of potatoes. Tuck or fold under overlapping side and top crust. Make a hole in middle of top crust. Combine the ⅓ cup hot water and the vanilla. Pour into hole, over potatoes. Bake 50 minutes. Add pats of butter to top crust. Increase oven temperature to 400°F. Brown crust for 5 to 10 minutes.

CRUST

2 cups all-purpose flour
½ teaspoon salt
⅓ cup butter or margarine
⅓ cup vegetable shortening
⅓ cup ice water

Mix the flour and salt in a large bowl. Work both the butter and shortening into flour with a pastry mixer. Bits of shortening should be pea size. Moisten the dough with the ice water by stirring with a fork.

—*Ms. Norma Foster*

Rhubarb Cobbler

When cooked, rhubarb takes on a beautiful deep red color that adds visual appeal to this delicious dessert. Don't skimp on the sugar, though; rhubarb can be as tart as the comment of a church lady.

MAKES 6 TO 8 SERVINGS

2 cups dry bread crumbs

1 cup butter or margarine, melted

2 cups tender rhubarb, cut into 1-inch pieces

Juice of one lemon

1 cup sugar

• • • Preheat the oven to 375°F. Grease a 3-quart baking dish. Toss the bread crumbs in butter until well coated. Combine the rhubarb and lemon juice. Sprinkle with ½ cup of the sugar. Place a layer of rhubarb on the bottom of the buttered dish. Cover with bread crumbs. Sprinkle with ½ cup of the sugar. Continue layering rhubarb and sugar and bread crumbs until all ingredients are used, ending with a layer of bread crumbs. Top with thin slices of butter. Cover with foil. Bake 40 minutes. Serve with a scoop of strawberry ice cream.

—Brenda Rhodes Miller

CHAPTER 3

Cookies and Candy

Mrs. Ruth Ferguson, serving a Good Friday plate at Mt. Airy Baptist Church, took orders for her cakes, pies, and dinners via e-mail.

Let the Circle Be Unbroken

Say the word *missionary* today, and most people think of someone who goes far away to spread the Gospel in a foreign land. Churches support the work of their foreign missionaries with prayer and love offerings of money, books, and clothes. In the old days, however, missionary groups were the original self-help organizations. Missionary Circles were composed of churchwomen whose charge was to help needy church members, be they the elderly and infirm, the sick and shut-in, or the widows and orphans.

These women did not go off to foreign countries, nor did they send money to support strangers in strange lands. Their job was looking out for people much closer to home. They would visit the sick, providing prayer and companionship. If the sick were at home, rather than in a hospital, the Missionary Circle would provide meals, and they might also do the washing, clean house, go shopping for groceries, administer medication, and stand in for an inattentive family member.

When the Great Migration separated families into southern and northern branches, Missionary Circles also helped the church to attend to members who might have no relatives living nearby.

Today, many churches support the work of foreign missions, while Missionary Circles continue to draw church members who believe that charity begins at home.

Easy Buttery Cookies

Because this dough handles well, prepare ahead of time, bring leaf-shaped cookie cutters, and invite your Sunday school nursery class to make this easy treat for their families.

MAKES 5 DOZEN

4 cups all-purpose flour
1 cup packed light brown sugar
1 pound butter, softened

• • • Preheat the oven to 325°F. Combine the flour and sugar in a large bowl, mixing well. Add the butter and mix well. Place the mixture on a floured surface and pat to ½-inch thickness. Cut into desired shapes. Place on a baking sheet. Bake for 20 to 25 minutes. Cool on wire racks before storing in airtight containers.

—Mrs. Luevenia Combest

Short'nin' Bread Cookies

Black History Month celebrations are a good time to introduce these cookies and the song that goes with them.

MAKES 2½ DOZEN 2-INCH SQUARES

1 large egg
1 cup sugar
2 cups cold butter or margarine
4 cups all-purpose flour

• • • Preheat the oven to 350°F. Whip the egg and sugar together in a large bowl until smooth. Cut in the butter. Cut in the flour, a little bit at a time. Turn the dough out onto sparsely floured waxed paper. Form dough into a ball that sticks together. Divide into two portions and slightly flatten. Dust waxed paper with flour. Gently roll dough to ¼ inch thick. Cut into squares. Put on buttered cookie sheet. Bake 10 to 12 minutes or until light golden brown. Store cooled cookies in an airtight container.

—Dr. Willie Creagh Bolden

Drop Sugar Cookies

These are good cookies to make for Vacation Bible School snacks.

MAKES 6 TO 7 DOZEN

½ cup shortening

½ cup butter or margarine

2 cups sugar

3 eggs

1 cup buttermilk

3½ cups all-purpose flour

2 teaspoons baking soda

2 teaspoons baking powder

• • •Preheat the oven to 375°F. Cream the shortening, butter, and sugar in a large bowl. Add the eggs and buttermilk; mix well. Combine the flour, baking soda, and baking powder in a medium bowl; mix well. Stir into creamed mixture. Drop the batter by rounded teaspoons about 2 inches apart on a greased or nonstick cookie sheet. Bake 10 to 12 minutes or until golden brown. Remove to wire racks to cool.

—adapted from Edith Barber's Cookbook *and* Inglenook Cookbook

Butter Nut Cookies

Depending on what's available, you can substitute pecans or peanuts for the walnuts. Adults and children will enjoy these cookies.

MAKES 4½ DOZEN

3 cups all-purpose flour

8 tablespoons sugar

⅞ pound butter

1 teaspoon vanilla

½ pound walnuts, finely ground

Powdered sugar

• • •Preheat the oven to 300°F. Combine the flour and the sugar in a large bowl; mix well. Add the butter, vanilla, and walnuts. (The dough will be crumbly, so use enough additional flour, if needed, to obtain a consistency that you can roll into walnut-size balls.) Bake 25 to 30 minutes or until golden brown. While the cookies are still warm, shake them in a paper bag filled with powdered sugar. Cool and store in an airtight container.

—Mrs. Beulah Hughes

Jewels

These pretty little cookies look just perfect on a lace paper doily at a church bake sale. Use several different colors of jam to get the real jewel effect.

MAKES 1½ DOZEN COOKIES

½ cup butter or margarine, softened
¼ cup packed light brown sugar
1 large egg, separated
1 teaspoon vanilla
1 cup all-purpose flour, sifted
1 cup finely chopped walnuts or pecans
2 tablespoons strawberry preserves or preserves of your choice

• • • Combine the butter, sugar, egg yolk, and vanilla in a medium bowl using an electric mixer; mix until smooth. Stir in flour just until combined. Refrigerate about 30 minutes. Preheat the oven to 375°F. Roll the dough into balls about 1 inch in diameter. Dip in slightly beaten egg white, then roll in walnuts. Place 1 inch apart on ungreased cookie sheets. With thimble or thumb, press center of each cookie. Bake 10 to 12 minutes or until golden brown. Remove to wire rack to cool. Place ¼ teaspoon preserves in center of each cookie.

—Ms. Beverly Crandall

Basic Tea Cakes

It used to be that tea cakes—really little decorated cookies—were favorites at every occasion. Every church baker has a special secret tea cake recipe. This one adds a little bit of spice.

MAKES 3 DOZEN COOKIES

½ cup butter-flavored shortening
½ cup sugar
1 large egg
1 teaspoon vanilla
2 cups all-purpose flour
2 teaspoons baking powder
¼ teaspoon baking soda
¼ teaspoon salt
¼ cup buttermilk
3 teaspoons sugar
½ teaspoon nutmeg or 1½ teaspoons cinnamon

• • • Preheat the oven to 375°F. Combine shortening and the ½ cup sugar in a large mixing bowl. Beat at medium speed with an electric mixer until light and fluffy. Beat in the egg and vanilla. Combine the flour, baking powder, baking soda, and salt in a separate large bowl, then add to the creamed mixture alternately with the buttermilk; mix well after each addition. Form the dough mixture into a ball; chill for 1 hour in the refrigerator. Roll the dough to ¼-inch thickness on a lightly floured surface. Cut with a floured 2½-inch round cookie cutter or glass jar. Place on a greased baking sheet. Combine the 3 teaspoons sugar and the nutmeg or cinnamon in a small bowl, mixing well. Sprinkle over the top of each tea cake. Bake for 7 to 9 minutes. Remove to a cooling rack. Serve warm or at room temperature with your favorite cup of hot tea.

NOTE: You can substitute almond or lemon flavoring for the vanilla in the batter. These cookies are best if eaten on the first day.

—Family and Friends Favorite Recipes *and* The Black Family Dinner Quilt Cookbook

dentation. Work it together. Add milk, a little at a time, working together until you get the consistency of a biscuit dough. Place dough on a bread board sprinkled with all-purpose flour. Roll into a large loaf and cut into 1-inch-thick cookies. Press down with a lightly greased spatula. Fill the cookie sheet. Bake about 10 to 12 minutes, or until brown. Cool on a wire rack. Store in a tin lined with waxed paper.

—*Ms. Joyce A. Fourth*

Tea Cake Cookies

Delicious and easy to prepare, this tea cake recipe is slightly different from the preceding one and has a milder flavor.

MAKES 2 TO 2½ DOZEN CAKES

2 cups self-rising flour
2 large eggs
½ cup soft butter or margarine
½ cup sugar
1 tablespoon vanilla
About ⅓ to ½ cup milk
All-purpose flour

• • • Preheat the oven to 350°F. Place the flour in a large bowl and make an indentation. Place the eggs, butter, sugar, and vanilla in the in-

Lemonade Tea Cakes

Frozen lemonade gives an unexpected flavor to this tea cake recipe and proof to the endless creativity of church ladies.

MAKES 5 TO 6 DOZEN

3 cups all-purpose flour
1 cup sugar
1 teaspoon baking soda
1 cup butter or margarine, softened
2 large eggs
1 (6-ounce) can frozen lemonade, thawed

• • • Preheat the oven to 400°F. Sift the dry ingredients together in a medium bowl. Cream the butter in a large bowl; add the eggs and mix well. Alternately add the lemonade and a small amount of the flour mixture until all is used. Drop by teaspoonfuls onto ungreased cookie sheet. Bake about 8 minutes or until slightly brown. Cool on wire racks.

—*Mrs. Philonese Thompson*

. . . .

Sour Cream Cookies

Nothing sour about these yummy cookies or the sweet missionary lady who bakes them for her circle! The sour cream makes them extra moist.

MAKES 6 DOZEN

1 cup butter or margarine
2 cups sugar
3 large eggs, beaten
1 teaspoon vanilla
1 cup sour cream
5 cups all-purpose flour
3 teaspoons baking powder
1 teaspoon salt
1 cup chocolate chips
Frosting (optional; recipe follows)

• • • Preheat the oven to 350°F. Cream together the butter and sugar in a large bowl. Add the eggs, vanilla, and sour cream; mix well. Combine the flour, baking powder, and salt in a medium bowl. Stir the flour mixture into the creamed mixture, mixing well. Stir in the chocolate chips. Place tablespoonfuls on greased cookie sheet. Flatten with fork. Bake

15 to 17 minutes. Remove to wire racks to cool. Frost, if desired. Serve warm or cooled.

FROSTING

1 (16-ounce) package powdered sugar
½ cup butter
2 teaspoons vanilla
2 teaspoons lemon juice
2 tablespoons milk

Combine all the ingredients in a medium bowl; mix well. Spread on cooled cookies.

—*Mrs. Lolita Cusic*

. . . .

Carrot Cookies

Sunday school teachers cut the tops off carrots and root them in a cup of water to show little children how things grow.

MAKES 3 DOZEN

¾ cup shortening
¾ cup sugar
2 large eggs
2 cups all-purpose flour
2 teaspoons baking powder
¼ teaspoon salt
1 cup cooked mashed, carrots
⅛ teaspoon nutmeg
1 teaspoon vanilla
Powdered sugar

• • • Preheat the oven to 350°F. Cream the shortening and sugar in a large bowl. Add the eggs, flour, baking powder, and salt. Stir in the carrots, nutmeg, and vanilla; mix well. Drop mixture by tablespoonfuls onto a baking sheet. Bake 20 minutes or until slightly brown. Sprinkle with powdered sugar while still warm.

—*adapted from* Inglenook Cookbook

Mama's Coconut Macaroons

As children, our job was to shred the coconut for these light and chewy cookies that Mama made as a special Sunday dinner dessert. Store cookies in an airtight container.

MAKES 24 MACAROONS

3 large egg whites
1 teaspoon vanilla
1 cup powdered sugar, sifted
¼ teaspoon finely ground nutmeg
1 cup shredded sweetened coconut

• • • Preheat the oven to 325°F. With an electric mixer, beat the egg whites and vanilla in a large bowl until soft peaks form. Gradually add the sugar and finely ground nutmeg. Continue beating until the egg whites are very stiff and all the sugar is incorporated. Gently fold in the coconut. Drop by rounded teaspoonfuls onto a greased cookie sheet (or drop onto

parchment paper). Place the cookie sheet on the middle rack in the oven. Bake 20 to 25 minutes or until the coconut is lightly browned. Slip the parchment paper onto a rack from the cookie sheet to cool. Store in an airtight container.

—*Brenda Rhodes Miller*

Quick Chocolate Drops

Patience is a virtue, but these are so good, you may not be able to wait. They taste great right from the freezer.

MAKES 4 DOZEN COOKIES

2 squares Baker's unsweetened chocolate, melted
1 (14-ounce) can sweetened condensed milk
2 cups chopped pecans or 3 cups shredded coconut

• • • Preheat the oven to 350°F. Combine the chocolate and condensed milk in a medium bowl. Stir in the chopped pecans or coconut; mix well. Drop by teaspoonfuls on a greased baking sheet. Bake for 15 to 18 minutes. Remove from pan immediately and cool on wire racks. Store extras in the freezer in sealed bags.

—Edith Barber's Cookbook

Keeping a Record

MRS. KATHERINE L. WINSLOW
Mount Joy Baptist Church
Washington, D.C.

Born and reared in Big Stone Gap, Virginia, Mrs. Katherine L. Winslow, like any other child of the South, had to belong to a church. So she joined First Baptist Church, an old congregation built more than eighty-five years ago. While at First Baptist, she sang in the choir and attended Sunday school and Baptist Training Union (BTU).

She received her early education in Big Stone Gap but finished her last year of high school in Concord, North Carolina, at Barber Scotia High School. Like millions of others from the South who wanted a better-paying job, she headed north—not too far north, though, just to Washington, D.C. The year was 1935. It was in Washington, D.C., where she met and married her husband, Edward Winslow, in 1937.

"I joined Mount Joy Baptist Church in October 1947. With me I brought my singing voice and my willingness to serve in any manner I could. I became the Envelope Clerk in 1950. My job was to distribute the dues envelopes to the members and to keep accurate records of what each member paid. Back then, tithing was virtually unheard of, which made my job easy because we didn't have to have any special envelopes for tithing, just for the regular offerings. I must have done a good job, because after a year, I was asked to be Church Clerk. I kept that job for thirty-eight years, working with three different pastors," recalls Mrs. Winslow.

She used the shorthand and typing she learned at night school, plus the skills she acquired working as a receptionist in a doctor's office, to do that. Part of her job was to keep things in order.

Enrolling new members was vital. She had to fill out the History Cards, get the members to sign them, and then file the cards. "Nobody knew any-

Though she retired from her duties as Church Clerk after 38 years of service, Mrs. Katherine Winslow continues to keep good records.

thing about computers back then; everything was done by hand, so it helped to have nice handwriting, and later on, to be a good typist. My record keeping included knowing how many people in a family belonged to the church, who got married, who died, and when a person was baptized, so that our records would be as accurate as possible. All this information helped me write the obituary and news for the church paper when a member died," says Mrs. Winslow. The church "paper," or newsletter, is still an important source of information for members.

She took the minutes at all business meetings, which then became part of the church history, which is still referred to today. Not only did she have to prepare the Sunday bulletin, but she also had to read it out loud during Sunday worship service. This courtesy is still provided in most churches to spare members whose failing eyesight or inability to read would otherwise keep them in the dark about church activities.

"In preparation for the bulletin," she says, "I had to know just about every single thing that was going on in the church, from meetings to fund-raisers, such as teas and fashion shows, to musical programs. In addition, I had to have everyone's telephone number, because sometimes people called me with news about events or with names for the sick and shut-in list, and I had to be able to tell them where to call to get more information. Seemingly, I was the one-woman yellow pages for the church. I loved my job as Church Clerk, and I gave it everything I had until I resigned in 1989."

Put off the youth choir because of her age, she joined the Number Two Usher Board in the early 1950s, and today she still shows people to their seats every first Sunday, along with being the recording secretary of the Usher Board.

Meringue Kisses

If you want to get fancy about it, add a drop of food color to the egg whites and make Meringue Kisses that match your bridal shower color scheme.

MAKES 4 DOZEN KISSES

3 large egg whites
¾ cup sugar, divided
Pinch of salt
½ teaspoon vanilla extract

• • • Preheat the oven to 275°F. Beat the egg whites until stiff peaks form in a large bowl. Beat in ½ cup of the sugar and the salt. Fold in the remaining ¼ cup sugar and the vanilla extract. Drop the mixture by teaspoonfuls on a nonstick or lightly greased baking sheet. Bake for 30 minutes. Remove from baking sheet and cool.

NOTE: Add ½ cup finely chopped almonds or pecans to the batter before baking, if desired.

—Edith Barber's Cookbook

Molasses Crinkles

Bake big batches of these spice-filled cookies to put in church holiday baskets for the nursing home ministry or to give as gifts to the sick and shut-in.

MAKES 3 DOZEN

¾ cup shortening or butter

1 cup packed dark brown sugar

1 large egg

4 tablespoons molasses

2¼ cups all-purpose flour

2 teaspoons baking soda

1 teaspoon ginger

1 teaspoon cinnamon

½ teaspoon salt

½ teaspoon cloves

½ teaspoon allspice

Additional granulated sugar

• • • Cream the shortening and the brown sugar in a large bowl until light and fluffy. Add the egg and the molasses, mixing well. Sift the dry ingredients, except the additional sugar, together; add to the creamed mixture, mixing well. Chill the dough for 30 minutes.

Preheat the oven to 375°F. Roll the dough into walnut-size balls. Roll in the sugar. Bake about 12 to 14 minutes. Cool on wire racks; store in an airtight container.

—Carol Martin

Crisp Cookies

Choir practice goes faster with the promise of a tasty finish like these cookies that are similar to gingersnaps.

MAKES 2 DOZEN COOKIES

1 cup dry unseasoned bread crumbs

½ cup packed light brown sugar

½ teaspoon salt

1 teaspoon ginger

½ teaspoon baking soda

2 large eggs, beaten

1 teaspoon melted butter

1 teaspoon vanilla

¼ cup molasses

• • • Preheat the oven to 350°F. Combine the bread crumbs, sugar, salt, ginger, and baking soda in a large bowl. Add the eggs, butter, vanilla, and molasses; mix well. Drop from teaspoon about 2 inches apart on a greased baking sheet. Bake for 15 minutes or until brown. Watch closely.

—adapted from The Southern Cookbook of Fine Old Recipes

Gingery Snaps

Sharp yet sweet, these cookies may remind you of things church ladies say when they think no one is listening.

MAKES 3 DOZEN

¾ *cup butter or margarine*

1 cup sugar

4 tablespoons light molasses

1 large egg

1 teaspoon cloves

1 teaspoon cinnamon

1 teaspoon ground ginger

2 cups all-purpose flour, sifted

2 teaspoons baking soda

Additional sugar

• • • Preheat the oven to 375°F. Cream the butter and sugar together in a large bowl. Add the molasses, egg, and spices. Add the flour and baking soda, mixing well. Form the batter into small balls about 1 inch in diameter. Roll the balls in sugar and place on a greased cookie sheet. Bake for 8 to 10 minutes.

—*adapted from* Inglenook Cookbook

Florida Cookies

Many churches celebrate "State Sundays" in recognition of the home states of their founding members. A church that boasts many members from Florida will enjoy this unusual cookie with its distinctive orange flavor.

MAKES 3 DOZEN COOKIES

¼ *cup butter or margarine*

¾ *cup sugar*

½ *cup orange juice*

Grated rind of 1 orange

1 large egg

3 cups all-purpose flour

2 teaspoons baking powder

Additional sugar

• • • Preheat the oven to 350°F. Cream the butter and sugar in a large bowl. Stir in the orange juice and rind. Add the egg, mixing well. Combine the flour and baking powder in a medium bowl. Stir into the creamed mixture. Place dough on a floured board. Roll dough to ⅛-inch thickness. Cut with cookie cutters. Place cut shapes on a baking sheet. Top with sprinkles of sugar. Bake for 12 minutes.

—*adapted from* The Southern Cookbook of Fine Old Recipes

Mentor to Young Mothers

MRS. NUNTIATA BUCK
St. Martin de Porres Church
Milwaukee, Wisconsin

Even when she was a little girl, Nuntiata Buck was a church lady. Mass on Sunday and Mass on first Friday, Morning Prayer, grace before and after meals, and the Rosary were all regular parts of her life. She belonged to a parish with its own school taught by nuns, and, like every Catholic schoolgirl, she learned the liturgical calendar.

Parish life is punctuated by saints' days, also known as feast days, and celebrations. Each one has its own rich traditions and its own colors: red for Pentecost, purple for penance, green for hope, blue for Mary.

In the fall were days honoring the dead. Then there was Advent, with its evergreen wreath and pink and purple candles. Midnight Mass on Christmas Eve was both a religious and a social event. In February came the feast of St. Blaise. No child wanted to miss the throat blessing, when the priest touched every neck with a pair of long white tapers, cool, heavy, unlit wax candles that seemed to soothe the scratchy throats of winter. Lent meant forty days of privation, when schoolchildren gave up candy to prepare their souls for Easter, the most important day of the church year. May was Mary's month, with special Masses and processions and dancing around the maypole in honor of the Mother of God

St. Martin de Porres, one of the few black saints of the church, was said to have the power of bilocation, a blessing that allowed him to be in two places at once. Today, Nuntiata Buck is a grown-up church lady who belongs to St. Martin de Porres Catholic Church, where she works with unwed mothers, helping them to develop plans for themselves and their babies. Her work includes teaching the girls how to make a budget, how to shop for food, and how to prepare nutritious meals. She is a mentor, giving the girls what all children need, a caring adult who believes in their possibilities.

Gourmet Chocolate Chip Cookies

Send young scholars who are away at college a box of these cookies to remind them of their home church.

MAKES 9 TO 10 DOZEN

2 cups butter or margarine,
  softened
2 cups granulated sugar
2 cups packed light brown sugar
4 large eggs, slightly beaten
2 teaspoons vanilla
4 cups all-purpose flour
5 cups dry oatmeal
1 teaspoon salt
2 teaspoons baking powder
2 teaspoons baking soda
24 ounces semisweet chocolate chips
1 (8-ounce) chocolate bar, grated
3 cups chopped walnuts

• • • Preheat the oven to 375°F. Cream together the butter, sugar, and brown sugar in a large bowl. Add the eggs and vanilla. Combine the flour, oatmeal, salt, baking powder, and baking soda in a large bowl; mix well. Mix dry ingredients with creamed mixture, blending well (batter will be stiff). Stir in the chocolate chips, grated chocolate bar, and nuts. Make golf ball–size dough pieces and place 2 inches apart on an ungreased baking sheet. Bake for 6 to 7 minutes. Remove to wire racks to cool. Store in an airtight container.

—*Mrs. Lolita Cusic and* Family and Friends Favorite Recipes

. . . .

Oatmeal Cookies

As comforting as a warm breakfast, these cookies are the favorite of many Usher Board members.

MAKES 6 DOZEN COOKIES

2 cups sifted all-purpose flour
¾ teaspoon baking soda
1 teaspoon salt
½ teaspoon cinnamon
½ teaspoon cloves
1 cup shortening
1½ cups brown sugar, firmly packed
2 large eggs, well beaten
1½ cups rolled oats
1 cup chopped walnuts or pecans
¼ cup buttermilk

• • • Preheat the oven to 325°F. Sift together the flour, baking soda, salt, and spices in a medium bowl. Cream the shortening in a large bowl; add the sugar slowly, and cream until fluffy. Stir in the eggs. Add the oats and the nuts, and mix well. Stir in the sifted dry ingredients alternately with the buttermilk. Drop by teaspoonfuls on a greased baking sheet and let stand a few minutes. Flatten dough with a fork or by stamping with a tumbler covered with a damp cloth. Bake 10 to 15 minutes.

—*adapted from* Edith Barber's Cookbook

. . . .

Coco-Oat Cookies

This recipe is a bake sale favorite, especially when made into extra large cookies.

MAKES ABOUT 5 DOZEN

1 cup butter or margarine
½ cup sugar
1½ cups packed brown sugar
2 large eggs
2 cups all-purpose flour
1 teaspoon baking soda
½ teaspoon salt
1½ teaspoons vanilla
2 cups rolled oats
1 cup coconut
12 ounces semisweet chocolate chips

• • • Cream the butter and sugars in a large bowl. Add the eggs, mixing well. Stir in the flour, baking soda, salt, and vanilla; mix well. Fold in the oats, coconut, and chocolate chips. Chill dough for 1 hour.

Preheat the oven to 350°F. Drop by rounded teaspoonfuls onto a greased cookie

sheet. Bake 15 minutes. Grease the sheet for each new batch of cookies. Cool on a wire rack.

—*adapted from* Inglenook Cookbook

. . . .

Easy Holiday Cookies

These no-bake nutty cookies are perfect to serve after Christmas Eve service.

MAKES ABOUT 6 DOZEN COOKIES

2 pounds white almond bark
1 cup smooth peanut butter
2 cups roasted peanuts
3 cups miniature marshmallows
3 cups rice cereal

• • • Melt the almond bark with the peanut butter in the top of a double boiler; cool 5 minutes. (**NOTE:** The cooling is very important, so the marshmallows won't melt.) Stir in the remaining ingredients; mix well. Drop by teaspoonfuls on waxed paper. Cool completely before storing.

—*Cynthia Moore*

. . . .

Cheesecake Bars

All the flavor of cheesecake in a bar cookie—
another church bake sale favorite.

MAKES ABOUT 1 DOZEN BARS

⅓ cup butter or margarine
⅓ cup packed dark brown sugar
1 cup all-purpose flour
½ cup finely chopped pecans
¼ cup granulated sugar
1 (8-ounce) package cream cheese
1 large egg
2 tablespoons milk
1 tablespoon lemon juice
½ teaspoon vanilla

• • • Preheat the oven to 350°F. Cream the
butter and brown sugar in a large bowl until
light and fluffy. Add the flour and the nuts;
blend until the mixture resembles crumbs,
and set aside ¾ cup. Press the remaining mixture into the bottom of an 8-inch square pan.
Bake for 15 minutes. Combine the sugar and
the cream cheese in a medium bowl; beat until smooth. Add the egg, milk, lemon juice, and
vanilla, beating well. Spread the cream cheese
mixture over the baked crust. Sprinkle the reserved ¾ cup of crumbs over the top. Bake for
25 minutes. Cool for 1 hour in the refrigerator
and cut into bars.

—Mrs. Vivian Hinds

Cream Cheese Squares

When church nurses have their monthly
meeting, someone is sure to bring this yummy
dessert.

MAKES 16 SERVINGS

1 cup all-purpose flour
½ cup packed dark brown sugar
⅓ cup butter or margarine
½ cup chopped pecans
1 (8-ounce) package cream cheese
1 large egg
¼ cup granulated sugar
2 tablespoons milk
2 tablespoons lemon juice
½ teaspoon vanilla

• • • Preheat the oven to 350°F. Combine the
flour, brown sugar, and butter in a medium
bowl. Stir in the pecans. Remove 1 cup of the
mixture; set aside. Press the remaining mixture into the bottom of an 8-by-8-inch pan.
Bake 8 to 10 minutes. Combine the cream
cheese, egg, granulated sugar, milk, lemon
juice, and vanilla in a medium bowl. Pour on
top of baked crust. Crumble reserved flour
mixture over top. Bake an additional 25 minutes. Remove from the oven. Cool on a wire
rack before slicing into squares.

—Mrs. Deloris Agee

Peanut Butter–Oat Bars

Who says healthy eating can't include sweets? Let the raves begin when you bring these fiber-filled bars to the meeting of the church Administrative Board.

MAKES 15 TO 18 SERVINGS

⅔ cup butter or margarine
1 cup packed dark brown sugar
4 cups quick-cooking oatmeal
3 teaspoons vanilla
½ cup light corn syrup
1 cup chocolate chips
⅔ cup crunchy peanut butter

• • • Preheat the oven to 350°F. Cream the butter and sugar in a large bowl. Add the oatmeal, vanilla, and corn syrup. Mix well. Pat dough into a greased 13-by-9-inch baking pan. Bake for 16 to 18 minutes. While cooling slightly, melt chocolate chips and peanut butter in the top of a double boiler. Spread on dough and cool thoroughly. Cut into bars.

—Carol Martin

Pecan Turtle Bars

Even though there isn't much for the Garden Ministry to do in the dead of winter except decide about spring plantings, serving these delicious bars will keep the members coming to meetings.

MAKES 24 SERVINGS

2 cups all-purpose flour
1½ cups packed brown sugar, divided
½ cup + ⅔ cup butter or margarine,
    softened
1 cup chopped pecans
1 cup milk-chocolate chips

• • • Preheat the oven to 350°F. Combine the flour, 1 cup of the brown sugar, and ½ cup of butter in a large bowl; mix at medium speed for 2 to 3 minutes. Press into a greased 13-by-9-inch baking pan; sprinkle with pecans. Combine the remaining brown sugar and butter in a medium saucepan; cook over medium heat for 1 minute; stir constantly. Pour the mixture over pecans. Bake for about 20 minutes or until caramel is bubbly and crust is golden. Sprinkle with chocolate chips; let stand until melted, then swirl chocolate over surface. Cool and cut into bars.

—Mary Ellen Robinson

Banana Bars

The buttermilk and bananas make these bars moist and tasty high-energy treats.

MAKES 4 DOZEN

1 stick butter or margarine,
   softened
1½ cups sugar
2 large eggs
1 cup whole-wheat flour
1 cup all-purpose flour
½ teaspoon salt
1 teaspoon baking soda
¾ cup buttermilk
1 teaspoon vanilla
3 ripe bananas, mashed
Powdered sugar

• • • Preheat the oven to 350°F. Cream the butter, sugar, and eggs in a large bowl. Sift together the flours, salt, and baking soda. Add the buttermilk and flours alternately to the butter mixture. Add the vanilla and banana; mix thoroughly. Spread into greased jelly-roll pan and bake 30 minutes. Cool. Dust with powdered sugar. Cut into bars.

—Brenda Rhodes Miller

• •

Square Toffees

Keep these on hand for unexpected company after church, or when you get assigned at the last minute to bring a dessert to a meeting. These squares freeze well, so you can carry them to a function. By the time you're ready to enjoy them, they'll be ready to eat.

MAKES 2 DOZEN LARGE SQUARES

1 cup packed dark brown sugar
1 cup butter or margarine
2 cups all-purpose flour
1 cup semisweet chocolate chips
1 cup chopped pecans

• • • Preheat the oven to 350°F. Cream the sugar and the butter in a large bowl. Add the flour; mix well. Stir in the chocolate chips and the pecans. Press into a 10-by-15-inch baking dish. Bake 30 to 35 minutes. Cool. Cut into squares.

—Carol Martin

• •

Butterscotch Bars

If you've given up candy for Lent, these quick-and-easy bars with the texture of a cookie may satisfy your sweet tooth.

MAKES 24 BARS

1 stick butter or margarine, softened
2 cups packed light brown sugar
2 large eggs, lightly beaten
1 cup all-purpose flour
1 teaspoon baking powder
½ cup chopped pecans
1 teaspoon vanilla
Powdered sugar

• • • Preheat the oven to 350°F. Cream the butter and the sugar in a large bowl; add the eggs and mix well. Sift together the flour and the baking powder. Add to the creamed mixture. Stir in the nuts and the vanilla. Spoon the mixture into a greased and floured 13-by-9-inch pan. Bake for 25 to 30 minutes or until done. Sprinkle with the powdered sugar. Cool, then cut into squares to serve.

—Family and Friends Favorite Recipes

Banana Oatmeal Cookies

Serve this cookie without guilt. It is both delicious and nutritious!

MAKES 4 DOZEN COOKIES

⅔ cup butter or margarine, softened

2 large eggs

1 cup mashed bananas, divided

1½ cups sifted all-purpose flour

1 cup sugar

1 teaspoon cinnamon

1 teaspoon baking powder

¼ teaspoon baking soda

¼ teaspoon nutmeg

Pinch of salt

1½ cups rolled oats

• • • Preheat the oven to 375°F. Combine the butter, eggs, and half the bananas in a large bowl. Beat until creamy. Combine the flour, sugar, cinnamon, baking powder, baking soda,

nutmeg, and salt in a large bowl; mix well. Add to the creamed mixture. Fold in the oats and the remaining bananas, mixing well. Drop the mixture from a teaspoon onto a greased cookie sheet. Bake about 15 minutes or until lightly browned around edges. Cool before storing.

NOTE: Adding ½ teaspoon banana extract gives additional flavor. Adding ½ cup chopped pecans gives additional texture.

—Family and Friends Favorite Recipes

Fruitcake Cookies

Even if you're not a fan of fruitcake, you're likely to enjoy this cookie. The texture and the taste are both exceptionally appealing. The contributor has celebrated fifty years as a Sunday school teacher and her one hundredth birthday.

MAKES 9 DOZEN COOKIES

1 cup packed dark brown sugar

½ cup butter or margarine, softened

4 large eggs, slightly beaten

3 teaspoons milk

3 cups all-purpose flour plus extra for
     dusting fruit and nuts

2 teaspoons baking soda

1 teaspoon ground cinnamon

1 teaspoon ground cloves

1 teaspoon ground nutmeg

¾ cup rum

1-pound total of combination of chopped
   candied red cherries, green cherries,
   figs, apricots, and pears
1 pound dates, chopped
4 cups pecan halves

••• Preheat the oven to 275°F. Cream the sugar and the butter in a large bowl. Add the eggs, mixing well after each addition. Stir in the milk. Sift together the flour, baking soda, cinnamon, cloves, and nutmeg in a large bowl. Add to the creamed mixture. Stir in the rum. Lightly flour the cherries, dates, and pecans. Fold into the batter. Drop by teaspoonfuls onto lightly greased baking sheets (or use parchment paper–lined baking sheets). Bake for 30 minutes. Remove to a wire rack to cool.

—Mrs. Beulah Hughes

Little Lemon Fruit Cakes

The contributor got this recipe from her grandmother, Maria White, who sang spirituals and hymns as she baked.

MAKES 7 TO 8 DOZEN

1 pound butter, softened
2½ cups sugar
6 large eggs
3 ounces lemon extract
4 cups all-purpose flour

½ teaspoon salt
1 pound chopped candied cherries
½ pound chopped candied pineapple
½ pound white raisins
1 pound pecan pieces

••• Preheat the oven to 325°F. Cream the butter and sugar in a large bowl. Add the eggs, one at a time, beating well after each addition. Add the lemon extract and blend. Sift the dry ingredients together in a large bowl; add to the creamed mixture. Stir in the fruit and nuts. Spoon the mixture into well-greased 1¾-ounce soufflé or nut cups, filling each three-fourths full. Place on baking sheets. Bake for 30 to 35 minutes. Test for doneness using a straw or knife. Cool slightly and remove from cups.

—Ms. Joyce Felder

Praline Brownies

This sweet brownie has the taste of fabled New Orleans pralines.

MAKES ABOUT 36 BROWNIES

½ cup packed dark brown sugar
¾ cup butter or margarine, divided
2 tablespoons evaporated milk
½ cup coarsely chopped pecans
2 cups packed light brown sugar

2 large eggs

1½ cups all-purpose flour

1 teaspoon vanilla extract

½ teaspoon salt

• • • Preheat the oven to 350°F. Combine the dark brown sugar, ¼ cup of the butter, and the evaporated milk in a small saucepan. Cook over low heat just until the butter is melted, stirring constantly. Pour into an ungreased 8-inch square baking pan. Sprinkle evenly with the pecans.

Cream the light brown sugar and the remaining ½ cup butter in a large bowl. Add the eggs, mixing well. Stir in the flour, vanilla, and salt, mixing just until moistened. Spread the batter over the pecans, making sure to cover crust completely. Bake for 45 to 50 minutes or until the brownies test done. Remove pan to a cooling rack; cool for 5 minutes. Invert the pan onto a tray or serving platter. Cool completely before cutting into squares. Cover as soon as brownies cool.

—*Ms. Diana R. Weekes*

Chocolate Brownies

Who can have a church bake sale without brownies?

MAKES 2 DOZEN

⅔ cup sifted all-purpose flour

½ teaspoon baking powder

¼ teaspoon salt

6½ tablespoons butter or margarine, melted

2 squares unsweetened chocolate, melted

1 cup sugar

2 large eggs, well beaten

1 teaspoon vanilla

½ cup chopped walnuts

• • • Preheat the oven to 350°F. Combine the sifted flour, baking powder, and salt in a large bowl; sift together. Combine the butter and the melted chocolate in a medium bowl; blend well. Cream the sugar and the eggs in a medium bowl. Add to the chocolate mixture. Combine the creamed mixture and the flour mixture. Stir in the vanilla and walnuts. Pour into a greased 8-by-8-inch baking pan. Bake for 35 minutes. Cool on a wire rack. Cut into squares before removing from the pan.

—*Ms. Melanie Shelwood*

Left Her Mark on the World

MRS. MARIA WHITE
St. John on Gray "off Dowling"
Houston, Texas

In the early 1930s, Maria and Moses White, with daughter Juanita, standing in the church house door.

The old song "Somebody Prayed for Me" tells a story that resonates with many twenty-first-century church ladies.

> *Somebody prayed for me,*
> *Got down on their knees,*
> *Took the time and prayed for me.*
> *I'm so glad they prayed, I'm so glad they prayed,*
> *I'm so glad they prayed for me.*

Take Joyce Felder, for example. She is a retired federal government executive who belongs to a prominent congregation where she was formerly a member of the trustee board. The church recently completed a ten-million-dollar renovation on its historic sanctuary.

This is a far cry from the church of her childhood. Her grandparents, Maria and Moses White, were part of the early migration of poor blacks who moved from Louisiana to Texas in search of opportunity. In the 1920s her grandfather was the first to venture out, seeking a home for his wife and his daughter Juanita, Joyce Felder's mother. The family settled in Houston, where they immediately joined Rose Hill Baptist Church. Her grandfather became an usher and an officer of the church. Her grandmother served with the Courts of Callenthe, which was the ladies' auxiliary. "It was my grandmother who taught me my prayers. I learned the old words of the Lord's Prayer, the 'trespass' version, not the 'debtor' version I say today," she explains. "Nanny also taught me to bless the sick and afflicted in my prayers. I know she prayed for me all the time because she told me so."

Mrs. White was also a wonderful cook, and her coconut cake with pineapple filling is one of Joyce Felder's fondest special-occasion memories. "Unfortunately, I don't have *that* recipe, but I do have Nanny's recipe for Little Lemon Fruit Cakes."

The Christmas after her grandmother's death, Joyce made dozens of the cakes and sent them to her grandmother's friends and to a family for which she had worked. "People sent me notes of heartfelt love for Nanny, telling me what she had meant to them as they thanked me for the cakes. It made me feel so connected to Nanny, I felt like I was reclaiming part of my heritage."

Her grandmother taught her many important lessons, not the least of which is the power of prayer. "I don't recall her having a remarkable voice, but it seemed she was always humming a song of Jesus' love and grace as she cooked or worked in the garden she so dearly loved. She was always praying for somebody—very often, me—and I try to follow her example. It is the least I can do."

Peanutty Brownies

These double crunch brownies are sure to be a favorite with the church sports teams.

MAKES 3 SERVINGS

½ cup crunchy peanut butter
⅓ cup butter or margarine
¾ cup packed light brown sugar
¾ cup sugar
2 eggs, slightly beaten
2 teaspoons vanilla
1 cup all-purpose flour
1 teaspoon baking powder
Pinch of salt
1 cup chopped pecans

• • • Preheat the oven to 350°F. Combine the peanut butter, butter, and sugars in a large bowl; beat until light and fluffy. Add the eggs, one at a time; beat well. Stir in the vanilla and set aside. Combine the flour, baking powder, and salt in a medium bowl. Slowly add to peanut butter mixture. Stir in the pecans. Spread the batter into a 13-by-9-inch baking pan. Bake for 25 to 30 minutes. Cool and cut into squares.

—*Joyce A. Fourth*

. . . .

Cherries and Chocolate

Yummy and easy to make, this dessert should be part of every church bake sale.

MAKES 3 DOZEN

1 cup sifted all-purpose flour
⅓ cup packed light brown sugar
½ cup butter or margarine
¼ teaspoon salt
18 maraschino cherries, well drained and halved
6 (1-ounce) squares semisweet chocolate, melted

• • • Preheat the oven to 350°F. Combine the flour and sugar in a large bowl. Cut the butter and salt into the flour mixture until it resembles a pie dough. Press it into an 8-by-8-inch baking pan. Bake for 20 minutes. While it is warm, cut it into 36 squares. Cool and place them in a pan lined with waxed paper. Place a cherry half on each square and cover each cherry with a spoonful of melted chocolate. Chill squares for a few minutes until the chocolate hardens.

—*Carol Martin*

Marshmallow Treats

Talk about gilding the lily! This is a novel way to elevate the lowly marshmallow to regal status!

MAKES 2½ DOZEN

2 squares of semisweet chocolate
1 (14-ounce) can sweetened condensed milk
2 cups graham cracker crumbs
1 teaspoon vanilla
1 cup chopped walnuts
30 large marshmallows (about half of a
    1-pound bag)
1 cup flaked coconut

• • • Melt the chocolate in the top of a double boiler. Add the milk, cracker crumbs, vanilla, and walnuts. Mix well. Remove from the heat and let cool slightly. Take marshmallows, one at a time, and fold mixture around them. Pour a single layer of coconut on a sheet of waxed paper. Roll coated marshmallows in coconut and let cool on a buttered plate in refrigerator. Cut in half when cool.

—*Mrs. Lolita Cusic*

Stained Glass Candies

Modern technology makes this recipe a whole lot easier than in the old days. Praise the Lord!

MAKES 40 TO 50 PIECES

½ cup butter or margarine
1 (12-ounce) package semisweet chocolate
    morsels
1 (10-ounce) package colored miniature
    marshmallows
1 cup pecans, chopped
2 to 2½ cups shredded coconut or powdered
    sugar

• • • Place the butter in a 3-quart casserole. Microwave on High for 1 minute, or until melted. Add the chocolate morsels. Microwave on Medium for 3 to 3½ minutes, or until the chocolate is melted. Cool the chocolate enough so that marshmallows won't melt when stirred in. Add the marshmallows and nuts. Allow to stand until stiff enough to form into rolls.

Spread the coconut or powdered sugar on two 1½-feet-long sheets of waxed paper. Divide marshmallow mixture in half. Form in

The Christian Journey

MS. VYLLORYA EVANS

Westminster Presbyterian Church

Washington, D.C.

When one begins the Christian journey, only God knows where it might end. Vyllorya Evans began her journey in Aberdeen, Mississippi, where she grew up in a Baptist church. From then to now, she has visited many churches of many denominations, tarrying awhile in some of them, looking for a place where her spirit might be fed and she could offer her service.

Huge mega-churches leave her cold—too many people, too impersonal, too hard to forge a connection—but she has been steadfast in her search for a church she could call home. In Dallas, she found Oak Cliff Presbyterian Church, which had a commitment to social justice and social change. The minister was a local leader who worked to prevent "white flight" and helped to maintain the stability of the neighborhood.

When Ms. Evans moved to Washington, D.C., she began her search anew, finally finding a small Presbyterian church in the southwest quadrant of the city with multiple, creative ministries that spoke to her heart. Contemporary stained-glass windows incorporating themes that reflect the national capital adorn the church. They were created by people like Ms. Evans who participated in stained-glass workshops conducted by the church. This is not the only ministry in which she has found her place to serve. Today, she is an officer in the Southwest Renaissance and president of Southwest Catering, a ministry that trains neighborhood people for jobs in the booming food-service industry.

In addition to caring for their spiritual health, the church attends to the physical health of its members and neighbors through an organized exercise program.

According to Ms. Evans, "Whatever the church I'm in, it has prepared me and helped me get ready for the next stage in my life. God always leads me where I need to be, so I am prepared for the next phase."

long rolls on the coconut or sugar. Coat all sides of rolls evenly. Store in the refrigerator until firm. Cut the rolls into ¼- to ½-inch slices.

NOTE: If the chocolate mixture hardens too much to roll out, microwave on Medium for 1 to 1½ minutes, or until softened.

—Cynthia Moore

Fudge

Who doesn't love the taste of homemade fudge? Make this recipe for passing out at as consolation prizes at Friday night Bingo!

MAKES ABOUT 30 SMALL SQUARES

¼ pound (1 stick) butter or margarine
¼ cup milk, divided
3 tablespoons unsweetened cocoa powder
1 (16-ounce) package powdered sugar, sifted
1 teaspoon vanilla
1 cup miniature marshmallows
½ cup coarsely chopped walnuts

• • • Slice the butter or margarine into pieces and place in a medium saucepan. Add half the milk and the 3 tablespoons cocoa. Cook over high heat for 2 minutes, stirring constantly. Stir in the powdered sugar; beat until smooth. Add the vanilla, marshmallows, and walnuts. Cook for 1½ minutes, beating until smooth. If mixture is too stiff, add enough of the remaining milk, one drop at a time, until the mixture

pulls away from the sides of the pan. Pour into a greased 8-by-8-inch pan. Allow the mixture to cool before cutting into squares.

—Mrs. Margie M. Holmes

Cocoa Fudge

The contributor has raised thousands of dollars for her church by selling this fudge at parish events. Yummy!

MAKES 8 TO 10 MEDIUM SQUARES

3 cups sugar
⅔ cup unsweetened cocoa powder
⅛ teaspoon salt
⅔ cup evaporated milk
½ stick butter or margarine
1 teaspoon vanilla
¾ cup chopped pecans

• • • Combine the sugar, cocoa, and salt in a large saucepan; mix well. Add the milk and bring to a boil over medium heat, stirring often. Add the butter; boil, while stirring, until a small amount of mixture dropped in cold water forms a ball. Remove from the heat. Stir in the vanilla. Beat until thickened. Stir in the pecans. Spread in a 8-by-5-inch greased pan. Cut into squares after fudge sets.

—Mrs. Margie M. Holmes

Church Candy

MRS. MARGIE M. HOLMES
Prince of Peace Catholic Church
Mobile, Alabama

Just about anybody can give a little money to the church. Raising a lot of money is much harder, but it's something Mrs. Margie Holmes has managed to do with great results for the past twenty years. She started her amazing candy sales when her church asked every member to buy a brick for one hundred dollars. With heavy tuition bills for her children in school, an extra hundred dollars was hard to come by, so this resourceful church lady decided to sell candy to raise the money.

Her candy is something special, and in no time flat she sold enough to buy her brick. From there, it was a simple step to start making candy all the time and donating the proceeds to her church. When the church has its festival, all the members have to do is put up a sign announcing that Mrs. Holmes's candy will be for sale, and in a matter of hours, she sells out all the candy she's made.

Here's how she works. People collect pecans from their trees and bring them to her. In November, she sets up her cracker at the kitchen table and starts picking out the nutmeats for the candy. In years when the pecan crop is good, she and her family also collect nuts from their own trees. They might pick out ten, twenty, or thirty gallons. When the crop isn't so good, she has to buy pecans, which adds to the cost of her candy making.

Nuts secured, she starts making candy right after Easter, giving herself a month to make the fudge and pralines that are so beloved their sales have netted thousands of dollars over the years. Mrs. Holmes makes only two kinds of candy, fudge and pralines, because those are the candies she likes. "I don't care for divinity, so I don't try to make it." In addition to the pecans, parishioners also donate sugar, cocoa, cream, and other ingredients so that all the candy she makes is pure profit for the church.

The hardest part is standing over the stove stirring and stirring, but for Mrs. Holmes, it is a labor of love. "Once I get going, I don't stop until I've finished making all the candy," she says. "I usually sell out before I'm even set up good."

In the nearly twenty years she's been making candy for her church, she's probably raised more than ten thousand dollars. "I intend to keep doing it until I can't do it anymore. When people come up to me and tell me they want my candy, I feel good knowing I'm making them happy and making money to help the church, too."

Brown Sugar Fudge

Nothing beats the taste of this candy.

MAKES 2½ DOZEN

2 tablespoons butter or margarine
¾ cup milk
1½ cups sugar
1 cup packed light brown sugar
1 teaspoon vanilla
1 cup chopped pecans

• • • Melt the butter in a 2-quart saucepan. Add the milk and the sugars. Cook over medium heat, stirring until the sugars are dissolved. Test by feeling the back of the wooden spoon while stirring the mixture. You should not feel any granulated sugar. Cook, covered, for 1 minute. Uncover and cook gently about 15 minutes or until a small mixture dropped in cold water forms a soft ball. Remove from the heat and cool until the outside of the pan feels lukewarm to the touch. Stir in the vanilla and nuts. Beat with a spoon until the mixture loses its gloss. Press into a greased 8-by-8-inch baking dish. Cut into squares.

—*adapted from* Inglenook Cookbook

Chocolate Turtles

This is an old-fashioned turtle. Most modern turtles have paraffin, which changes the taste and look. These homemade candies come out firm and chewy.

MAKES 50 CANDIES

3 cups pecan halves
50 caramels
12 (1-ounce) semisweet chocolate
    baking squares

• • • Preheat the oven to 300°F. Arrange the pecan halves in groups of threes, flat side down, on three greased baking sheets. Place a caramel on top of each cluster. Place the baking sheet in the oven until the caramels soften (about 5 to 7 minutes). Remove the baking sheet from the oven and flatten the caramels over the pecans with a buttered spoon. Cool slightly. Melt the chocolate in the top of a double boiler over simmering water. Place each turtle on a spoon and dip it into the chocolate, making sure both sides are well coated. Cool on waxed paper. When the chocolate hardens, store in a cool place in an airtight container.

—**Family and Friends Favorite Recipes**

Pralines I

Southern pralines are a traditional church festival candy—always delicious, no matter how many calories they might include!

MAKES ABOUT 24 PRALINES

2 cups powdered sugar
½ cup cream
1 cup maple syrup
2 cups chopped pecans

• • • Combine the sugar, cream, and maple syrup in a large saucepan. Bring to a boil. Cook until a small amount dropped in cold water forms a soft ball (238°F). Cool and beat until creamy. Stir in the pecans. Drop by teaspoonfuls onto greased waxed paper (this is important because mixture is sticky). Let cool.

—Rumford Complete Cookbook

Pralines II

These scrumptious candies have a fudgelike texture and are popular as holiday gifts.

MAKES 30 PRALINES

1 cup packed dark brown sugar
1 cup granulated sugar

½ cup evaporated milk
½ stick butter or margarine
2 cups chopped pecans

• • • Combine the sugars and the milk in a medium saucepan. Cook, stirring often, until the sugars dissolve. Add the butter, stirring until a soft ball forms when a small amount is dropped in cold water. Remove from the heat; beat until the mixture thickens. Stir in the nuts. Drop by teaspoonfuls on greased waxed paper. Let cool.

—Mrs. Margie M. Holmes

Brown Sugar Treats

Why buy ready-made candy for church sales when homemade candy is so easy to prepare?

MAKES 24 TO 30 SERVINGS

2 cups packed dark brown sugar
½ cup milk
1 tablespoon butter
1 cup chopped walnuts or pecans

• • • Combine the sugar and milk in a medium saucepan over medium heat. Cook, stirring constantly, until the sugar dissolves. Add the butter; bring to a boil. Continue boiling until a small amount of the mixture forms a ball when dropped into cold water (238°F). Remove from the heat. Stir in the nuts and beat mixture well. Spoon into a greased 9-inch baking pan. Cool and cut into squares.

—adapted from Rumford Complete Cookbook

. . . .

Peanutty Peanut Butter Candy

A cross between a cookie and a candy, this delicious recipe will bring smiles to all who taste it.

MAKES ABOUT 10 DOZEN

1½ *cups all-purpose flour*
½ *cup butter or margarine*
¾ *cup packed dark brown sugar*
⅛ *teaspoon salt*
1 *(12-ounce) package peanut butter chips*
1½ *tablespoons butter or margarine*
1½ *cups water*
¼ *cup light corn syrup*
1½ *cups salted peanuts*

• • • Preheat the oven to 375°F. Combine the flour, ½ cup butter, brown sugar, and salt in a large bowl; cut with pastry cutter until mixture is crumbly. Pat into a 13-by-9-inch pan. Bake 10 minutes. Combine peanut butter chips, 1½ tablespoons butter, water, and corn syrup in the top of a double boiler; cook over medium heat until melted. Add the peanuts. Remove the pan from the oven. Spread the

mixture over the crust. Return to oven, and bake 8 minutes longer. Loosen edges from sides of pan while warm. Cool. Cut into 1-inch squares.

——Carol Martin

. . . .

Chocolate Nut Candy

Make batches of this candy and put in pretty boxes for Valentine's Day gifts at church.

MAKES 8 DOZEN (1-INCH) BALLS

2 *(16-ounce) packages powdered sugar*
1 *(14-ounce) can sweetened condensed milk*
1 *stick butter or margarine, softened*
1 *teaspoon vanilla*
4 *to 5 cup chopped pecans*
Coconut, if desired
1 *(4-ounce) block paraffin wax*
4 *(2-ounce) squares bittersweet chocolate*

• • • Combine the powdered sugar, condensed milk, butter, vanilla, pecans, and coconut, if desired, in a very large bowl; mix well, using your hands. Form the mixture into balls and lay on waxed paper. Heat the paraffin and chocolate in a heavy saucepan until chocolate melts (do not bring to a boil); cool about 3 minutes. Using a bamboo skewer, tip the pan and dip the pecan balls into the chocolate sauce, twirling the skewer as you dip. Hold up to cool, then dip again. Remove with your fingers and lay on waxed paper to cool.

—*Mrs. Don't-You-Dare-Use-My-Name*

. . . .

Whiskey (or Rum) Balls

Christmas season is incomplete without rum balls.

MAKES ABOUT 5 DOZEN

1 pound vanilla wafers
2 cups chopped pecans
2 tablespoons unsweetened cocoa powder
3 tablespoons light corn syrup
6 jiggers (about 6 ounces) whiskey or rum
Sifted powdered sugar

• • • Crush the vanilla wafers in a large bowl or on waxed paper using a rolling pin. Stir in the pecans, mixing well. Stir in the cocoa. Add the syrup; mix well. Add the whiskey; mix well. Form the mixture into small balls. Let stand for 5 minutes. Coat with the powdered sugar. Store in a large glass jar with extra powdered sugar.

—*Mrs. Rita Stebbins*

. . . .

Sea Foam

A light and lovely sweet. Make it just for special ladies' events at church.

MAKES 40 SMALL SERVINGS

1 egg white
2 cups packed light brown sugar
½ cup water
1 teaspoon vanilla extract
½ cup chopped pecans

• • • Beat the egg white in a medium bowl until stiff peaks form; set aside. Combine the sugar and water in medium saucepan. Bring to a boil, and continue cooking for about 7 minutes or until a small amount dropped in cold water forms a soft ball (238°F.). Pour the hot mixture over the egg white, beating vigorously until the candy stiffens, about 2 to 3 minutes. Stir in the vanilla and the nuts. Drop by teaspoonfuls on waxed paper. Remove from paper when cool.

—*adapted from* Inglenook Cookbook

. . . .

Spiced Pecans

Put out a bowl of these on Christmas Eve and watch them disappear!

MAKES 1½ CUPS

1 cup sugar
1 teaspoon cinnamon
¼ cup evaporated milk
2 teaspoons water
1 teaspoon rum flavoring
1½ cups pecan halves

● ● ● Combine the first 5 ingredients in a saucepan over medium heat. Stir often. Let mixture come to a rolling boil for 5 minutes. Remove from heat. Stir in pecans to coat with syrup. Leave pecans in syrup for 10 minutes. Pour onto a well-greased sheet of waxed paper. Separate pecans with a fork. Let cool. Store in an airtight container. Eat as a snack or use as an ice-cream topping.

—*Mrs. Juanita H. Eaton*

CHAPTER 4

Custards and Puddings

*Church nurses at Mt. Joy Baptist Church in Washington, D.C.,
ready to assist worshipers.*

A Cooling Hand on a Fevered Brow

Church nurses have a big job. In addition to providing basic first aid such as stopping nosebleeds and bandaging cuts and scrapes, they may monitor members' blood sugar levels, administer insulin, and check blood pressure. They "see to" elderly members and console the bereaved, prostrate with grief at funerals. Often, they bring the pastor hot tea with lemon and honey before he preaches and juice when he sits down.

Dressed in their neat white uniforms and nurses' caps, they perform their most visible and well-established function during worship service. Church nurses stand ready to aid worshipers who are overcome by the Spirit.

When the Holy Spirit moves through a church, men and women may cry or dance the holy dance; some will rock to and fro with joy; they may begin to jerk and shake in spasms of religious excitement. A few people will run up and down the aisles; some will stand up to sing, speak loudly, or testify; others may faint or begin speaking in tongues. These demonstrations of religious fervor fall under the heading of "shouting" or "getting happy" or even being "slain in the Spirit." When church people "get the Holy Ghost," it is time for the nurses to kick into high gear.

A Baptist preacher reported that once, during a particularly exuberant worship service, a handful of worshipers fainted dead away. All over the church, the nurses sprang into action. Cold water splashed on the faces of some members revived them. Bottles of smelling salts held under the noses of others brought them back to their senses. But burning paper waved around one woman's head had no effect; even light slaps to her face failed to bring her around. Only when one elderly nurse got the pastor's nod to remove her shoe and hold it over the face of the afflicted did the poor woman rouse herself and come back to the land of the living. Since a preacher tells this story, we must assume it is true.

When a person gets carried away in the Spirit, nurses must exercise judgment about how long to wait before they intervene. Many experienced nurses simply pray while the Spirit works until the worshipers are exhausted. Some nurses immediately go stand near people who are in the Spirit, fanning them and offering water. Others grab and hold onto the Spirit-filled person to keep him or her safe from harm. When a nurse wraps her arms around a thrashing worshiper, nearly wrestling the poor soul to the ground, the struggle might remind the uninitiated or the newly saved of a nightclub bouncer tackling an unruly patron.

There are old-school nurses who take a more direct approach. One venerable, no-nonsense church nurse, spry for her age, used to carry a folding Chinese fan with metal edges. When church members consistently got carried away in the Spirit at the same point in the service every single Sunday, she would rush to the nearest one's side and whip out her fan.

Her fast and furious fanning nearly always "accidentally on purpose" included smacking the worshiper smartly on an area of exposed skin. If her fan maneuver got the person's attention and interrupted the "shout," the nurse's withering glance was enough to send the worshiper skulking back to his seat. If her smack made no impression, she would continue to fan and soothe the person until the religious ecstasy abated. These maneuvers never failed to separate the wheat from the chaff.

Bread Pudding with Whiskey Sauce

This is a wonderful old-style recipe for those wanting to try a boiled bread pudding. The boiled pudding has a more "dumpling" or "rice pudding" texture and taste. It is well worth the time it takes to watch it boil.

MAKES 6 TO 8 SERVINGS

18 slices white bread, with crusts removed
½ cup milk
1 teaspoon cinnamon
1 teaspoon salt
1 tablespoon all-purpose flour
3 large eggs, lightly beaten
1 cup seedless golden raisins
¼ cup butter or margarine, softened
Dash cinnamon (optional)
Whiskey Sauce (recipe follows)

• • • Soak the bread in the milk in a large bowl for 10 minutes. Add the cinnamon, salt, flour, eggs, raisins, and butter. Mix the ingredients with your hands or with a heavy spoon until the dough is thick and smooth. Form into a large ball. Dip a large dishcloth or double thickness of cheesecloth in boiling water. Spread the cloth flat on a table. Sprinkle with flour. Place the dough in the middle of the cloth and tie the ends together. Suspend the pudding in boiling water in a large kettle, making sure the cloth does not touch the bottom of the kettle. You can tie the cloth to the kettle handles or suspend it on a large utensil over the kettle. Cook pudding in a slow boil for about 2½ hours, making sure to replace water as it boils away. Remove the cloth-wrapped pudding from the water and let stand 20 minutes before taking pudding out of cloth and placing it in a serving bowl. Add a dash of cinnamon, if desired. Pour the hot Whiskey Sauce over the pudding before serving.

WHISKEY SAUCE

4 tablespoons butter or margarine, melted
1 tablespoon all-purpose flour
3 tablespoons water
3 tablespoons whiskey
⅓ cup sugar
¼ teaspoon salt

Combine the butter and flour in a medium saucepan. Add the water, whiskey, sugar, and salt; stir well. Simmer for 10 minutes, stirring constantly. Pour over the hot pudding.

NOTE: This sauce can be made ahead of time and kept warm in a covered double boiler over hot, not boiling, water.

—*adapted from* The Southern Cookbook of Fine Old Recipes

Z's Bread Pudding

Pray your guests will save a bite of this delicious bread pudding for you!

MAKES 6 TO 10 SERVINGS

1 stick butter or margarine

4 large eggs

1 pint butter pecan–flavored liquid coffee
*   creamer*

½ pint heavy whipping cream

2 teaspoons vanilla extract

3 tablespoons bourbon

⅛ teaspoon cinnamon

Dash of nutmeg

6 cups French or Italian bread, cut into cubes

½ cup raisins

½ cup chopped pecans

• • • Preheat the oven to 350°F. Combine butter, eggs, coffee creamer, whipping cream, vanilla, and bourbon in a large bowl; mix well. Add the cinnamon and nutmeg, mixing well. Pour enough of the mixture into an 8-by-12-inch baking pan to cover the bottom. Add a layer of bread cubes over the creamed mixture. Sprinkle with one-third of the raisins and pecans. Repeat the layering process two more times until all ingredients are used. Let stand for about 7 minutes to allow the bread to soak up some of the liquid. Cover the pan with aluminum foil. Bake for 35 to 40 minutes. Remove the foil, and bake for an additional 5 minutes to lightly brown top of pudding. Cool.

Serve with French vanilla, butter pecan, or rum raisin ice cream.

—Zoë Marie Isaac Gadsen

Caribbean Bread Pudding

Received top honors in our test kitchen, and that's the God's honest truth. (You can find Coco Lopez in your grocery store with the drink mixes.)

MAKES 10 TO 12 SERVINGS

1 (24-ounce) loaf of stale white bread,
*   torn into pieces*

2 cups evaporated milk

1 (15-ounce) can Coco Lopez or cream
*   of coconut*

2½ cups sugar

4 large eggs, beaten well

¼ cup melted butter or margarine

2 teaspoons cinnamon

2 teaspoons nutmeg

2 teaspoons vanilla

• • • Preheat the oven to 275°F. Put the torn bread into a well-greased 3-quart baking dish. Combine the remaining ingredients in a medium bowl; mix well. Pour the mixture over the bread and press down with a spoon until the liquid is soaked into the bread. Bake 1½ hours or until the pudding is set and top is lightly browned. Test by inserting knife in center; it should come out clean. Serve warm with whipped cream, if desired.

—*Ms. Melanie Shelwood*

. . . .

Trifle

Trifle is the perfect dessert for a fancy event. Display it using your nicest cut-glass or crystal bowl and be prepared for lots of compliments.

MAKES 8 TO 10 SERVINGS

2 large eggs

1 tablespoon sugar

1½ cups scalded milk

1 teaspoon vanilla

½ pound ladyfingers

6 macaroons

½ cup sherry

¼ pound blanched almonds, chopped

¼ pound candied cherries and pineapple,
  chopped

1 cup whipped cream

2 tablespoons powdered sugar

• • • Prepare the boiled custard by beating the eggs slightly in top of a cool double boiler. Add the sugar and mix well. Stir in the scalded milk slowly. Place top over bottom of double boiler and cook over medium heat until the mixture coats the spoon, about 10 minutes. Remove from the heat and stir in the vanilla. Line a glass serving bowl with a portion of the ladyfingers. Break the remaining ladyfingers and macaroons into small, coarse pieces and place in the glass serving bowl. Cover with the sherry. Add the chopped nuts and fruit; mix together. Pour the boiled custard over the ladyfinger mixture. Cool until ready to serve. Whip the cream in a medium bowl with the powdered sugar until stiff peaks form. Top the bowl with the sweetened whipped cream.

—*Ms. Dora Finley*

. . . .

Fruit and Nut Pudding

MAKES 8 TO 10 SERVINGS

½ cup water

1 cup sugar

4 large egg yolks, beaten

1 pint cream, whipped

1 teaspoon vanilla extract

⅓ teaspoon almond extract

1 cup mashed, cooked chestnuts

1 cup raisins

½ cup canned peaches, cut up

½ cup crystallized cherries, cut up

• • • Combine the water and the sugar in medium saucepan. Bring to a boil; reduce heat and simmer for 5 minutes. Pour over egg yolks in the top of a double boiler, beating constantly while pouring. Cook over medium heat, stirring constantly, until mixture thickens. Strain and set aside. When the mixture is cool, stir in the whipped cream, the extracts, and the chestnuts. Pour into a mold and set in the freezer until slightly stiff. Fold in the raisins, peaches, and cherries. Return to the freezer until solid. Remove from freezer and defrost slightly before removing from mold.

—adapted from Rumford Complete Cookbook

Here, There, Everywhere

MRS. LUEVENIA COMBEST AND MRS. VIRGINIA STRONG
formerly of White Oak Missionary Baptist Church
Winnsboro, South Carolina
now of Norbeck Community Church
Silver Spring, Maryland

Mrs. Luevenia Combest and her older sister, Mrs. Virginia Strong, are not twins, but every Sunday they go to church dressed from head to toe in identical outfits. "We started dressing alike when we attended White Oak back in the fifties," reports Mrs. Combest.

Both sisters sing in the choir, Mrs. Strong being best known for her rousing rendition of "Shake the Devil Off." Her signature line is "If you let him ride, he's gonna want to drive," a reference to the Devil that she accompanies with the appropriate hand gestures and hip shimmies.

Sisters Luevenia Combest and Virginia Strong (also known as Moody and Chippie), celebrate the Church Homecoming.

Both sisters are beloved for the incredibly delicious pancakes they make after Sunday school or whenever the mood strikes them. Not trusting the utensils in the church kitchen, they bring their own electric griddles to church on Sunday, guaranteeing perfect pancakes every time.

Beautiful, full-figured women with ready smiles and unlined faces that give no clue as to their real age, the sisters will coyly admit only to being "old enough to know better." Both can make a stone chuckle with their steady stream of one-liners. Miss Virginia, also known as Chippie, Ginny, or Big Emma, is a major-league flirt. She once told her young pastor's wife, "I love your husband better than Peter loved the Lord. Mind you take good care of him. If you don't, I'll take him home with me anytime he wants to go."

Mrs. Combest, whose nickname is Moody, is no slouch herself when it comes to flirting. When a very handsome nineteen-year-old came to church on Mother's Day, she marched right up to him and, in the presence of his mother, announced, "If I were two or three years younger, I'd give you a run for your money." She made this declaration with one manicured hand on her hip.

The Turner sisters grew up in Winnsboro, South Carolina, and attended White Oak Missionary Baptist Church Number One, where they still return for the annual Homecoming Celebration. Winnsboro is a small country town with churches tucked away in the back

Every church fashion show must feature hats as model Luevenia Combest shows here.

roads, including at least one other White Oak Church, as well as a Weeping Mary Baptist Church. Some say there's also a Weeping Mary Don't You Mourn Church back in the woods, but that's hard to prove.

In Winnsboro, the Turner family farmed and raised lots of sweet potatoes. This abundance is the reason the two sisters know how to make more desserts with sweet potatoes than most. One of their specialties is sweet potato cobbler.

Mrs. Combest delights in gently teasing her older sister. "I tell people all the time that Ginny's my mother!" When asked how it is that her older sister has so many nicknames, Mrs. Combest can't wait to tell tales out of school.

"Well, let me see. We call her Ginny, because her Christian name is Virginia. That's plain enough. But the name Big Emma takes some explaining. There was a lady named Emma Tucker who came to our church. Miss Emma was a little, short woman, normal sized, but she could eat forever and never get fat. Ginny was always tall for her age and she ate a whole lot, just like Miss Emma. So to tease her, we started calling her Big Emma and the name stuck."

Mrs. Combest got her own nickname because she was the youngest of twelve children. As such, she says she was spoiled rotten and acted so moody all the time that her family just started to call her Moody.

In a farm family of six girls and six boys, storytelling was a favored form of entertainment. Not only can Moody weave a yarn better than most; she also knows scores of poems by heart. Each Sunday of Black History Month, she shares poems and stories during eleven-o'clock worship service.

The rest of the year, she tells stories on her sister. "One of the ladies in our church, her family owned the juke joint down the road. We lived just past the fork in the road and we'd sit on the porch Saturday night watching the cars drive to the left. Every time a car went that way, we'd say, 'Oh shoot!' They were on their way to the juke joint, not to see us. Our girlfriends who lived down the road would come sit with us, and when it came time for them to go home, we'd walk them 'piece the way' home. Soon as Ginny got past the lights of our house, she'd take off running to the juke joint. Everyone there would say, 'Oh here's Chippie Turner!' She'd get herself a dance and then run back where we were waiting for her. Then, on Sunday, our mother would say to Mrs. Harrison, the lady who ran the juke joint, 'Did you have a good crowd last night?' And Mrs. Harrison would answer, 'Oh, yes, ma'am, we did. Chippie was there, too.' Mother wouldn't say anything, but when we got home, Ginny would get a whipping. But she never did stop going to get her dance."

Chippie and Moody display genuine affection for each other that spreads to the entire congregation as they go about their devoted church service. Neither sister will disclose the genesis of the nickname Chippie, but they're quick to tell you they are founding members of the local blues society.

Carrot Pudding

Looking for a way to get your family to eat more vegetables without a fight? This tasty pudding may be just the ticket.

MAKES 8 TO 10 SERVINGS

2 tablespoons butter or margarine
1 cup sugar

2 large eggs
1½ cups grated carrots
½ teaspoon ground cloves
½ teaspoon cinnamon
¼ teaspoon nutmeg
¼ teaspoon salt
1 cup all-purpose flour, sifted
Grated rind of 1 orange
Grated rind of 1 lemon
1 teaspoon baking soda

1 cup grated white peeled potatoes
¼ pound thinly sliced citron

• • •Cream the butter and sugar in a large bowl. Add the eggs; beat well. Stir in the carrots, cloves, cinnamon, nutmeg, and salt. Stir in the flour, rinds, baking soda, and potato. Stir in the citron, mixing well. Butter a mold and place a sheet of greased waxed paper on the bottom. Pour in the pudding. Cover the mold and place it in a pot of boiling water to steam for 1 to 1½ hours. Serve warm with cream or your favorite sauce.

—*adapted from* The Southern Cookbook of Fine Old Recipes

Caramel Custard

Looking for a simple, comforting dessert? This one surely fills the bill.

MAKES 6 TO 8 SERVINGS

¾ cup sugar, divided
3 tablespoons water
4 cups milk
4 large eggs
1 teaspoon vanilla

• • •Preheat the oven to 350°F. Heat ¼ cup of the sugar with the water in a large cast-iron skillet until the mixture turns a rich dark brown. Cool. Scald the milk in a small saucepan and cool to lukewarm; pour the milk into the caramel liquid. Beat the egg yolks and egg whites together in a medium bowl. Add the remaining ½ cup sugar and the vanilla. Stir in the milk gradually. Pour the mixture into a 1-quart greased Pyrex dish. Place the dish in a deep pan. Carefully pour hot water into the pan but do not get the water into the custard. Bake for about 35 minutes, or until custard sets.

—*adapted from* Tante Marie's French Kitchen

Rice Pudding

When the Seniors' Ministry meets, try this coarse version of rice pudding that is not overly sweet.

MAKES 4 TO 6 SERVINGS

2 cups cooked rice
½ cup light brown sugar
3 tablespoons butter or margarine, melted
1 cup milk
3 large eggs, slightly beaten
½ cup raisins
½ teaspoon vanilla
Dash of nutmeg

• • •Preheat the oven to 350°F. Combine the rice, brown sugar, butter, milk, and eggs in a large bowl. Spoon the mixture into a well-greased 1½-quart baking dish. Bake for 30 minutes. Remove from the oven. Stir in the raisins and vanilla; sprinkle with the nutmeg. Bake for an additional 30 minutes. Serve warm or cold.

—*adapted from* The Southern Cookbook of Fine Old Recipes

. . . .

Floating Islands

A lovely old-fashioned dessert beloved by elderly church members, Floating Islands are both beautiful to behold and sinfully good.

MAKES 4 TO 6 SERVINGS

2 cups milk
3 tablespoons plus ⅓ cup sugar
⅛ teaspoon salt
4 large egg yolks, well beaten
1 teaspoon vanilla extract
½ teaspoon lemon extract
3 large egg whites
3 tablespoons lemon juice

• • • Scald the milk, 3 tablespoons of the sugar, and the salt in the top of a double boiler. Slowly add the beaten egg yolk to the hot milk. Strain the mixture, then return to the double boiler. Cook slowly (medium to medium-low heat) over an inch of simmering water, stirring constantly until the custard

coats a metal spoon. (Make sure mixture does not overheat or it will curdle.) Remove the mixture from the heat; stir in the extracts. Pour into a serving bowl or into individual custard cups; chill.

Before serving, preheat the oven to 375°F. Beat the egg whites until fluffy. Slowly add the remaining ⅓ cup sugar, beating well until sugar is dissolved. Add the lemon juice and continue beating until the whites are stiff. Fill a baking dish with cold water; drop egg whites by spoonfuls into the water. Bake 10 to 15 minutes or until the meringues are brown on top. Place meringues on custard. Serve immediately.

—*Ms. Daisy A. Voigt*

. . . .

Molded Pudding

MAKES 8 TO 10 SERVINGS

1 cup almonds
1 cup cold water
1 tablespoon plain gelatin
¼ cup water
1 cup sugar
1 cup milk
1 teaspoon lemon extract
Kiwi slices (optional)

• • • Force the almonds through a good processor, using the finest blade. With a mortar and pestle or a heavy potato masher in a bowl, pound the almonds while gradually adding the 1 cup cold water. Place the mixture in a dish towel and squeeze out the excess water. Place the mixture in a large bowl. Place the gelatin and the ¼ cup water in the top of a double boiler. Bring to a boil, stirring constantly, until the gelatin dissolves. Pour into the almond mixture. Add the sugar, milk, and lemon extract, mixing well until the sugar dissolves. Pour into a mold or dessert bowl. Chill for several hours. Unmold onto a chilled platter. Serve with slices of peeled kiwi, if desired.

—*adapted from* Inglenook Cookbook

Turn of the century members of the Church of God and Saints of Christ Tabernacle Number One in Washington, D.C. The lady is a distant relation of Ms. Voight.

Grandma Daisy's Berry Dumplings

Old fashioned dessert dumplings are becoming rare as stockings in the summertime.

MAKES 6 SERVINGS

1 quart blueberries or blackberries
½ cup sugar
¼ cup water
1 tablespoon lemon juice
½ teaspoon vanilla
1¼ cup all-purpose flour
2 teaspoons baking powder
½ teaspoon allspice
1 tablespoon sugar

½ teaspoon salt
2 tablespoons butter or margarine
¼ cup berries
⅔ cup milk

• • • Combine the 1 quart berries with the ½ cup sugar, the water, lemon juice, and vanilla in a 3-quart saucepan with a tight-fitting lid. Bring to a simmer and let cook covered for 5 minutes. Sift the flour, baking powder, allspice, sugar, and salt in a large bowl. Work the butter into the dry mixture. Add the ¼ cup of berries and the milk. Beat vigorously for about 1 to 2 minutes or until mixture is blended. Drop the dumplings by tablespoonfuls into the simmering berries. Cover the pan tightly and let simmer 35 minutes (do not open lid). Spoon dumplings into bowls and pour the juice over them.

—*Ms. Daisy A. Voigt*

. . . .

Prune Whip

Proof that things are seldom what they seem . . . in church or out . . . this fun and un-usual dessert looks like chocolate pudding—no one would guess it was prunes!

MAKES 8 TO 10 SERVINGS

1 cup sweetened, pitted prunes
1 cup water
1 teaspoon lemon juice
½ cup chopped pecans
1 pint whipping cream
1 cup powdered sugar
½ teaspoon lemon extract
Lemon peel curls for garnish

• • • Place the prunes and the water into a small saucepan. Bring to a boil; then cook slowly, uncovered, over medium heat for about 5 minutes. Cool in the pan. Puree in a blender or with an electric mixer. Combine the prunes and lemon juice in a medium bowl, mixing well. Stir in the chopped pecans. Beat the whipping cream, sugar, and lemon extract in a large bowl until stiff peaks form. Fold the prune mixture into the whipping cream. Spoon into stemmed glasses. Chill. Garnish with lemon peel curls.

NOTE: You can also spoon the whip into a baked 9-inch piecrust; chill. Garnish with lemon peel curls before serving.

—*Brenda Rhodes Miller*

. . . .

Coffee Cream

Like iced coffee, only fluffier and semisolid, this dessert can be enjoyed summer and winter. It's an ideal way to use leftover coffee from an early-morning deacons' meeting.

MAKES 4 TO 6 SERVINGS

3 large eggs
1½ cups milk
2 tablespoons plain powdered gelatin
⅔ cup strong coffee
½ cup sugar
1 cup whipping cream
Chocolate curls (use a vegetable peeler to
*   scrape curls from a bar of chocolate)*

••• Beat the eggs in the top of a double boiler; add milk and whisk together well. Cook until the mixture coats the back of a spoon, stirring while the mixture is cooking; remove from the heat and set aside. Soak the gelatin in the coffee in a small bowl for 10 minutes. Add to the egg mixture, which should be hot enough to dissolve the gelatin. Stir in the sugar, strain mixture through a sieve, and set aside to cool. Whip the cream until stiff. Add the cooled, strained-egg mixture gradually, folding carefully between each small addition. Spoon into a wet (5-cup) mold. Refrigerate until firm. Unmold on a serving plate. Serve with chocolate curls, if desired.

—*adapted from* Rumford Complete Cookbook

Easy Coffee Mousse

This mousse is almost too easy to be true. Make it when you don't have a lot of time but want to make a big impression.

MAKES 4 TO 6 SERVINGS

2 cups hot, strong black coffee
1 pound miniature marshmallows
1 cup heavy cream, whipped into soft peaks
Shaved chocolate

••• Pour the hot coffee over the marshmallows in a large bowl, stirring to dissolve the marshmallows. When the mixture is thick, gently fold in the whipped cream. Pour into individual glass serving dishes. Cover tops with waxed paper and refrigerate overnight. Serve garnished with the shaved chocolate.

—*Ms. Dora Finely*

Creole Charlotte Russe

Charlotte Russe is a traditional holiday dessert all along the Gulf Coast. Usually made just for special events at home, it can easily be transported for church celebrations as well.

MAKES 4 TO 6 SERVINGS

2 dozen ladyfingers (can substitute angel
 food cake or sponge cake)
2 cups Sweet Whipped Cream
 (recipe follows)
1 cup mixed chopped walnuts, almonds,
 and pecans
1 cup maraschino cherries, well
 drained and stems removed
½ cup mandarin orange sections,
 well drained

••• Grease a small serving bowl or other smooth round mold with unsalted butter. Press the ladyfingers into the bottom and sides of the mold. Prepare the Sweet Whipped

Cream. Combine the cream with the nuts, cherries, and oranges. Spoon into the lined bowl. Chill overnight. Unmold onto a doily-lined cake platter.

SWEET WHIPPED CREAM
2 cups heavy whipping cream
¾ cup powdered sugar
2 teaspoons coffee extract
1 tablespoon coffee liqueur

Beat the cream until it is thick but not dry. Stir in the sugar, coffee extract, and coffee liqueur. Use immediately.

—*Ms. Dora Finley*

CHAPTER 5

Frozen Treats

The sanctuary of this grand old church was full of family and friends during the funeral of an esteemed lady who was a beloved, lifelong member.

Feed the Soul by Feeding the Body

The final tribute most churches give departed members is the Repast. While not an official part of the Rite of Christian Burial, the Repast is a time-honored conclusion to funerals. Rare is the church that does not designate a group of church ladies to make sure this meal is served to mourners when they return from the cemetery.

After burying a loved one, the last thing a grieving family needs to worry about is feeding out-of-town friends and relatives. So, church members step in to cook and serve a huge meal, usually at the church, but sometimes at the home of the bereaved.

When the Repast is served at church, long tables are set and the food is put out cafeteria style with unlimited helpings available. The family sits at its own special table, fussed over and coddled by old friends, who bring heaping plates of food and insist that no matter how grief stricken one might be, "eating just a little something will make you feel better." In a way, the rich, heavy food and the loving attention act as sedatives, calming the overwrought and sustaining the exhausted.

The Repast served at home takes on a different character. It is a less formal meal, usually served buffet-style over the course of many hours. People may drop by and carry a plate home after they pay their respects to the family. It is a way to share in the grieving. Food and funerals have a powerful connection in the black community. As soon as the church learns a member has died, food starts appearing at the family home. Lots of food. Casseroles without number, hams, whole turkeys with dressing and string beans, fried chicken, vats of macaroni and cheese, barbecued ribs, loaves of bread, fancy frosted cakes, cobblers, pies, and simple pound cakes. In short, all the foods that might help bring comfort to the brokenhearted.

Other meals served at church may also be called repasts, but it is the food provided after a funeral that is always spoken of with a capital *R*.

Buttermilk Ice Cream

Don't let the name fool you, buttermilk ice cream is based on a sweet and rich cooked custard. Try it for the church Homecoming supper on the grounds.

MAKES 1 QUART

6 large egg yolks
¾ cup sugar
2 cups half-and-half
2 cups buttermilk

• • • In a small saucepan whisk together the yolks and the sugar. Cook over low heat, whisking constantly. Add the half-and-half gradually, whisking constantly, away from the heat. Return to the heat. Cook and whisk for 10 to 15 minutes or until the mixture coats the back of a wooden spoon. Do not boil. Remove from heat and strain mixture through a sieve into a bowl and refrigerate until cool. Whisk buttermilk into cooled custard until well combined. Add mixture to the fill line marking on ice-cream maker and freeze.

—*Mrs. Rita Stebbins and Ms. Beverly Mullens*

Peach Ice Cream

Only fresh, tree-ripened peaches will do for this delicious ice cream sure to be the star at the next church Ice Cream Social.

MAKES 6 QUARTS

1 quart heavy whipping cream
2 quarts whole milk
1½ cups sugar
2 tablespoons vanilla
1 cup ripe peaches, peeled and sliced

• • • Mix all ingredients, except peaches, in an ice cream freezer. Pack freezer with rock salt and crushed ice. Churn until nearly set frozen. Add peaches and stir. Put in coldest part of freezer for 1 hour before serving. For best texture, serve right from the churn.

—*Ms. Joyce Felder*

. . . .

Banana Ice Cream

The versatile banana makes splendid ice cream, a notch up from plain old vanilla.

MAKES 1 QUART

2 cups milk
2 cups heavy cream
2 large eggs, beaten
1¼ cups sugar
¼ teaspoon salt
1 cup pureed bananas
½ teaspoon vanilla extract
⅛ teaspoon nutmeg

• • • Combine the milk, cream, eggs, sugar, and salt in a large saucepan. Cook, stirring constantly, over low heat until the mixture thickens slightly and coats the back of a spoon. Refrigerate the mixture until it cools. Stir in the bananas, vanilla, and nutmeg. Pour into an ice cream freezer container. Freeze according to manufacturer's directions.

—*Mrs. Philonese Thompson*

. . . .

Very Berry Ice Cream

Hats bedecked with flowers and ice cream full of berries make outdoor summer church events extra special.

MAKES 2 QUARTS

½ pint strawberries
½ pint raspberries
1 pint blueberries
1½ cups sugar
3 tablespoons orange juice
4 cups light cream
1 teaspoon vanilla extract

• • • Combine the berries, sugar, and orange juice in a 3-quart saucepan. Mash the berries slightly and cook over medium heat, stirring occasionally, until the mixture comes to a boil; simmer 5 minutes. Remove from the heat and puree in a food processor or blender. To capture all the seeds, push the mixture through a fine strainer with the back of a wooden spoon; cool. Combine the berry mixture, cream, and vanilla in the chilled canister of an ice-cream maker; freeze according to manufacturer's directions.

—*Brenda Rhodes Miller*

. . . .

One Body, Many Members

MRS. EDWENA SEALS
Toulminville-Warren UMC
Mobile, Alabama

In the late sixties, a curious thing happened to the Methodist church in Alabama. As urban renewal destroyed old, established neighborhoods and the buildings in them, many thriving black congregations were left with no place to worship. Meanwhile, as social change became inevitable, many white congregations lost members as people raced from the city to the suburbs. The logical response was to put empty church buildings and full congregations together.

This is what happened to Warren Street Methodist Church, founded in 1889, and Toulminville Methodist Church, which were joined in 1966 to become the Toulminville-Warren Street Methodist Parish under co-pastors Rev. Joseph Griggs and Rev. Dallas Blanchard. In 1968, it became a United Methodist Church. Mrs. Edwena Love Seals is the church historian for the body.

Church historian Edwena Seals "styling and profiling" during the fifties.

Her mother, Mrs. Callie W. Love, had been the unofficial historian for Warren Street Methodist Church since joining in 1941. It was she who collected the photographs, programs, and records that formed the basis for the church history that Mrs. Seals wrote in 1996.

"I'd never been interested in history before. I studied it when I had to, but I didn't love history with a passion the way my mother did, and certainly not church history. She would visit any church that took her fancy, black, white, or green. It didn't matter. My mother just loved going to church and talking to people about their history. When we were children, she took us to all kinds of churches—Lutheran, Baptist, AME, and of course Methodist," Mrs. Seals recalls.

"When my mother died, I had so much material that I said, well, I'll go ahead and do this, write the church history. I went to the courthouse to get the names of the original trustees on the deed. Then I went to the census file to see if I could discover any of their descendants. The first good lead I got was a man who died the week after I got his name. The census file really got me interested, so I checked the telephone books. You won't believe how much information those old phone books have! Old phone books were more like school yearbooks, with write-ups about all the "important" people. Not only did they list names and addresses, but also lots of facts about the ministers, the district superintendent, and the bishops, including short biographies. The phone books were a gold mine."

Mrs. Seals is matter-of-fact about the difficulties she faced researching the history of the old Warren Street Church: "I tried the Central Alabama Conference that at one time maintained all the records of black churches. Before the white and the black conferences merged, the records, like everything else, were separate. Later, it turned out the North Alabama Conference had information on the ministers who served Warren Street." By dint of this hard work and perseverance, she has written a well-researched and informative history cherished by the church's members and other local historians.

Now, in the "new" church, established more than thirty years ago, Mrs. Seals continues her role as historian. The church historian is charged with making sure membership records are properly kept, and in consecutive order. Each baptismal record must include the full name and age of the child, the date of birth and date of baptism, as well as the names of the parents and the sponsors or godparents. Other membership records must list the legal name of the member who joins on the confession of faith, the name and former church of members who transfer their membership, and, of course, the date and name of the pastor. The church historian must also know where to find the confirmation lists, the minutes of trustee meetings, all property settlements, the marriage records of the church, and all legally binding documents.

"My job is to know where to find the records, not to keep the records myself," says Mrs. Seals, who works closely with the church secretary and the pastor. "Many of the old handwritten records are beginning to deteriorate," she laments. "I have spoken to archivists about preserving the artifacts of the church. I would love to start a church museum devoted to the history of this church, with exhibits, display cases of items donated by members, old photographs, and of course the records."

When Warren Street was razed in the late sixties, neither Mrs. Seals nor any of the members learned about the demolition in time to save any of the artifacts of the old church. "If only we could have saved the cornerstone," she sighs with the regret of a true historian.

Cherry-Macaroon Ice Cream

A ladies' luncheon following a fashion show in the church hall is the perfect occasion for this frozen treat.

MAKES 6 TO 8 SERVINGS

1 pint whipping cream
1 pint half-and-half
1 dozen macaroons
2 cups canned pitted cherries, with juice
Sugar to taste

• • • Whip the whipping cream until light peaks form. Add the half-and-half, mixing well. Crumble the macaroons and fold into the cream mixture. Mash the cherries. Add the cherries and juice to the cream mixture. Add sugar to taste. Place in shallow freezer container such as a metal ice cube tray without the dividers. Freeze for 1 hour. Remove from freezer and whisk briskly for 30 seconds. Return to freezer until ready to serve. When ready to serve, allow to soften slightly and spoon into parfait glasses.

—Carol Martin

Frozen Custard

Dress it up a bit with fresh diced fruit or add crushed vanilla bean.

MAKES 18 TO 20 SERVINGS

3 pints milk
6 to 8 large egg yolks, well-beaten
2 cups granulated sugar
1 cup packed light brown sugar
½ teaspoon salt
1 package unflavored gelatin
½ cup cold water
1 (12-ounce) can evaporated milk
1 pint cream

• • • Put 2 pints of the milk in the top of a double boiler; add the egg yolks, 1 cup of the granulated sugar, 1 cup brown sugar, and salt. Cook, while stirring, until the mixture coats a spoon. In another pan, heat the remaining 1 pint milk and the remaining cup of granulated sugar. Soak the gelatin in the cold water and then add to the second pan. Combine the two mixtures and add the evaporated milk and the cream. Place in a freezer container and freeze until solid.

—adapted from Rumford Complete Cookbook

Acting With Love

MRS. LUBERTA PORTIS
St. James Major Catholic Church
Prichard, Alabama

St. Peter Claver was a Spanish Jesuit who worked in South America to save the souls of enslaved Africans and abolish the slave trade in the seventeenth century. The entire fraternal body that bears his name, including the Knights, Ladies, Junior Daughters, and Junior Knights of St. Peter Claver, make up what is arguably the largest lay organization in the Catholic Church.

Mrs. Luberta Portis has been a member of the Ladies' Auxiliary for more than twenty-five years, holding local office as Chapter Grand Lady for ten years. She was also, at various times, president of the district, district deputy, and representative to the national board. During her tenure, thirteen new units were established in her district. She and her husband, who is a Knight, had the distinction of being the first married couple to sit on the national board.

"This is very much a family-oriented organization. We concentrate on education, service, and being good and faithful Catholics," she says.

Among the many activities run by the Ladies' Auxiliary is the "Soaring High" tutorial program that includes conducting after-school homework sessions and test-taking practice, providing meals, and giving whatever other assistance the children need to do well. The Ladies also give local and national scholarships to college-bound students.

"Before I became a member," Mrs. Portis explains, " seeing the Ladies in their white dresses made

an impression on me. Talking to them made me know they were doing something quite special within the church. They were really helping people.

"In 1980, when I became ill, it was then I learned the true meaning of membership. The Ladies visited me and did whatever I needed to have done. They brought fresh food, cooked meals for us, did the laundry, and they prayed with me. Every morning, one of them called me to see how I was doing.

"The Ladies perform Christian charity in the truest sense of the word. They act out of love."

Good Samaritans of Toulminville-Warren UMC preparing a holiday meal for sick and shut in members.

Cranberry Sherbet

An unusual and refreshing end to any meal, cranberry sherbet is a light alternative to heavy holiday desserts.

MAKES 8 SERVINGS

1 quart cranberries
2 cups water
1¾ cups sugar
Juice of 1 lemon
Juice of 1 orange

• • •Place the cranberries in a large saucepan; cover with the 2 cups water. Cook over medium heat until tender. Strain the berries through a fine sieve. Place in a large bowl and add the sugar and the fruit juices. Taste and add more sugar if needed. Stir well until the sugar dissolves; cool completely. Pour into a shallow freezer container and partially freeze. Place in a large chilled bowl and beat thoroughly with an electric mixer. Return to the freezer container and freeze completely.

—*Ms. Lois Ward*

Buttermilk Pineapple Sherbet

This sherbet is best when served right from the churn. Makes the perfect ending to the church league's softball tournament.

MAKES 4 QUARTS

½ gallon buttermilk
3 half pints whipping cream
8 ounces crushed pineapple, well drained
Juice of 2 lemons
2 tablespoons vanilla
About 3 cups sugar

• • •Combine the buttermilk, whipping cream, pineapple, lemon juice, and vanilla in a 5-quart ice cream freezer. Gradually add the sugar, tasting for the level of sweetness you like. Put the top on the freezer, add layers of salt and ice, and churn the mixture until firm. Put the freezer tub into the freezer until ready to serve.

—*Mrs. Rita Stebbins and Ms. Beverly Mullens*

Orange and Lemon Ice

Not too sweet, this heady ice has a terrific citrus flavor. For adults only.

MAKES 2 QUARTS

2 cups cold water

½ cup sugar

1 teaspoon grated lemon rind

½ cup lemon juice

1 cup freshly squeezed orange juice

6 tablespoons Grand Marnier or Cointreau
    liqueur, divided

• • • Place the water, sugar, and lemon rind in a medium saucepan; bring to a boil. Cook for 5 minutes; cool. Add lemon and orange juices; mix well. Place in a freezer container and freeze for 1½ hours. Remove from the freezer and beat in 2 tablespoons of the liqueur. Spoon into 4 sherbet glasses and return to the freezer until serving time. Float 1 tablespoon of the remaining liqueur over the ice in each glass before serving.

—*adapted from* Edith Barbour's Cookbook

CHAPTER 6

Specialty Desserts

A parade of choirs, followed by the entire congregation, marches through the neighborhood before returning to church for a Repast.

Make a Joyful Noise unto the Lord

Anytime a church can corral enough men to sing on a regular basis, jubilation fills the land. Churches struggle so hard to develop a male chorus or simply to fill the bass and tenor sections of the main choir that you'd think all the women in the choir stand were either invisible or mute. In the case of choirs, however, church ladies are both seen and heard. Choirs are built on the voices and efforts of church ladies. Not only do they sing, but they also organize, design robes, elect officers, run choir practice car pools, and influence the selections the choir will sing. They faithfully attend rehearsals, learn their parts, and give singing in a group their all. They are the mainstays of many choirs. Church ladies can always be counted on to make a joyful noise unto the Lord.

Beautifully robed, stepping off in unison down the center aisle, with pocketbooks clutched firmly in hand, church ladies lift their voices in song Sunday after Sunday. From the processional to the benediction, their voices are lifted as one.

Whether in the sanctuary of an established "silk stocking" congregation, where the singing is precise, or in an upstart "happy-pat" storefront where the same refrain may be repeated countless times, it is church ladies who are doing the singing. Naturally beautiful voices, rough, unpolished voices, terribly off-key voices, along with classically trained voices fill the ranks of choirs all over America.

The number of mega-churches increases daily, and those churches have huge choirs representative of their thousands of members. However, most churches in this country are still quite small, boasting only a few hundred members, if that. In fact, there are thriving congregations where if two hundred people all came to church at once it would be standing-room only.

Regardless of the congregation, a choir is central to the worship experience. In African-American churches good music, both vocal and instrumental, is a high priority. The choir and the musicians work cooperatively to bring the congregation closer to God through song. There are well-trained musicians and powerful choirs worshiping in many musical styles. But what a choir sings and how it sings in any particular church are important clues to what kind of church it has set out to be.

Mrs. Lucy Hall, First Lady of Friendship Baptist Church, Chicago, IL.

Some churches pride themselves on engaging accomplished pianists and organists who are comfortable playing classical music and anthems, to lend a solemn note of dignity to the worship service. These churches will want choirs with an exacting style of singing with even the variations carefully scripted. They will ring with traditional ecclesiastical music year round.

Others take a more contemporary approach, adding guitar, drum, and horn accompaniments to the traditional piano and organ. Their musicians will be as skillful as the traditionalists but will express a totally different style. These churches will draw on a growing body of contemporary gospel music to enliven their services and engage their members. Exuberant musical styles are attractive to worshipers who have rejected the staid music with which they grew up. But these churches are not the only ones who travel a different path.

Churches with deep roots in the rural South continue to praise God by singing spirituals in the old way, the moaning of the choir underscoring the meaning of the words. Other African-American churches, seeking to preserve the historical traditions and culture of communal worship, hearken back to the time when there were no instruments to accompany the choir. They celebrate the old styles, not heard very often these days, but always welcomed whenever someone takes a notion to lead the singing.

"Lining a meter hymn," for example, is where a single singer begins a song and after each line, the congregation follows, singing the words the lead singer has just sung for them. "Guide me, Great Jehovah, lead me through this barren land" lends itself to this style of singing as does "Come on in my room. Jesus is my doctor and he gives me all my med'cins and he writes down all my 'scriptions, in my room."

On the other hand, "harp singing" is more like a singing school class. The choir arranges itself in a square, organized into bass, soprano, alto, and tenor sections. The leader stands in the middle of the group and teaches them first to sing the notes and then the lyrics. Usually, the harp singer will use the do-re-me-fa-so-la-ti-do-named notes. The leader will take the group through the song several times using only the notes before moving on to teach them the lyrics. Harp singing is tremendously moving to hear.

"Call and response" is an ancient musical style with its roots in Africa. Similar to railroad crew and work gang singing, one voice sets the cadence and calls out a lyric. Then, the other voices respond with a lyric. An example of call and response is the song "Certainly, Lord." A lead singer asks, "Have you got good religion?" and the choir responds, "Certainly, Lord." The leader asks again, "Have you got good religion?" and after the third question, the choir responds, "Certainly, certainly, certainly Lord."

The great thing about church choirs is that even if one does not have a beautiful voice, there is still the opportunity to praise the Lord. Church choirs are infinitely forgiving, allowing bullfrogs and nightingales alike to participate. Most church choirs will take on anyone who wants to sing, giving one and all the chance to make a joyful noise unto the Lord. It is a rare blessing.

Apple Delight

Many people think Apple Delight is a kissing cousin to Apple Crisp. Serve it to guests at the church's fall festival supper.

MAKES 8 SERVINGS

5 large Rome Beauty or Red Delicious apples,
    peeled and chopped
½ cup sugar
1 tablespoon all-purpose flour
1 teaspoon nutmeg
¼ cup water
⅓ cup butter or margarine

5 slices stale white bread
Butter
¼ cup packed dark brown sugar
Vanilla ice cream or whipped cream (optional)
Mint sprigs (optional)

● ● ● Preheat the oven to 325°F. Place the apples, sugar, and nutmeg in a medium or large saucepan; mix well. Stir in the ¼ cup water and cover; cook slowly over low heat, stirring occasionally. Melt the butter in a 2-quart ovenproof baking dish. Toast the stale bread and crumble into the melted butter. Coat all the crumbs with butter. Toss the buttered crumbs with the brown sugar; remove from dish. Pour the apple mixture into the buttered ovenproof dish, and top with the sweetened bread crumbs. Bake 20 minutes or until the bread is brown. If desired, serve slightly warm with vanilla ice cream or whipped cream topped with a sprig of mint.

—Mrs. Lucille Battle

Church treasurer and usher Wendy Johnson spins cotton candy for the children during the fall festival at Norbeck Community Church.

Apple Strudel

Visiting choirs will appreciate this hearty fall dessert.

MAKES 8 TO 10 SERVINGS

6 baking apples, peeled and thickly sliced
2 tablespoons sugar
2 tablespoons cinnamon

Butter slices

1 cup sugar

1 teaspoon baking powder

1 cup all-purpose flour

1 large egg

• • • Preheat the oven to 350°F. Place thick layers of apples in the bottom of a well-greased 13-by-9-inch baking dish. Combine the 2 tablespoons sugar and 2 tablespoons cinnamon. Sprinkle over the apples and dot with butter.

Sift the 1 cup sugar, baking powder, flour, and salt in a medium bowl. Add the egg and mix until crumbly. Spoon over the apples. Bake for 20 minutes or until the crust is brown. Serve warm with milk, whipped cream, or ice cream.

—*Mrs. Luevenia Combest*

Pears in Honey Sauce

If you don't believe that simple pleasures are the best, one taste of Pears in Honey Sauce should convince you.

MAKES 6 SERVINGS

6 fresh uniform-size pears

⅓ cup sugar

⅓ cup water

¼ cup honey

3 tablespoons brandy

• • • Peel the pears and core, but leave whole. Combine the sugar and water in a large, deep skillet. Heat, stirring constantly, until the sugar dissolves. Stir in the honey. Add the pears, poaching them over low heat until tender but still hold their shape. Cool the pears in the syrup, basting occasionally. Stir in the brandy. Serve the pears and sauce in chilled dessert dishes.

—*Ms. Nicale Portis*

Dessert Pizza

Children love to help make this easy and colorful dessert. Try a combination of ripe peaches, plums, and nectarines for a delicious and healthy treat.

MAKES 8 TO 10 SERVINGS

1 stick butter or margarine

1 cup all-purpose flour

¼ cup powdered sugar

1 (8-ounce) package cream cheese

½ cup sugar

Fresh fruit slices of your choice

• • • Preheat the oven to 350°F. Combine the butter, flour, and powdered sugar in a food processor. Process until dough forms a ball. Press dough into a 12-inch pizza pan. Bake for 15 minutes; cool. Combine the cream cheese and sugar in a small bowl. Spread on the cooled crust. Top with a combination of fruit slices. Chill until ready to serve.

—*Mrs. Luevenia Combest*

. . . .

The Quad

No need to pretend you don't like dessert when this magnificent four-layered concoction is offered! It has something for everyone.

MAKES 10 TO 12 SERVINGS

1 cup butter or margarine, melted
1 cup all-purpose flour
1½ cups chopped pecans, divided
1 (8-ounce) package cream cheese,
   softened
1 cup powdered sugar
1 cup frozen whipped topping, thawed
2 (3-ounce) packages butterscotch or other
   flavored instant pudding
4 cups milk
Additional frozen whipped topping,
   thawed

• • • Preheat the oven to 350°F. Combine the butter, flour, and 1 cup of the pecans in a small bowl; mix well. Press into a 13-by-9-inch baking pan. Bake 20 minutes; set aside to cool. Combine the cream cheese, powdered sugar, and 1 cup whipped topping in a bowl. Spoon over the cooled crust. Combine the pudding mixes and milk in a large bowl; mix

well. Refrigerate for 5 minutes to help set. Spread over the cheese mixture. Top with additional whipped topping and the remaining ½ cup chopped nuts. Refrigerate until ready to serve.

—*Mrs. Dorothy McNeil*

. . . .

Ambrosia

Truly heavenly served either as dessert or salad.

MAKES 8 TO 10 SERVINGS

1 (20-ounce) can pineapple chunks in juice,
   drained
1 (11-ounce) can mandarin oranges, drained
1 cup shredded coconut
1 medium firm banana, sliced
1½ cups red grape halves
½ cup chopped pecans
1 cup miniature marshmallows
1 cup sour cream
1 tablespoon light brown sugar

• • • Combine the pineapple and the oranges in a large bowl. Stir in the coconut, banana, grapes, pecans, and marshmallows. Combine the sour cream and the brown sugar in a small bowl. Fold into the fruit. Refrigerate for 1 hour or overnight before serving.

—*Mary Ellen Robinson*

. . . .

And a Little Child Shall Lead Them

MRS. DOROTHY MCNEIL
Second New Saint Paul Baptist Church
Washington, D.C.

If the dictionary had to show the perfect illustration for "mother hen," it would be a picture of Mrs. Dorothy McNeil. Dottie, as she prefers to be called, is in almost perpetual motion. She fusses over people and the things that affect them. When Dottie is in charge of a meeting, first she inquires about everyone's health, then she begins adjusting the lights, offering chairs, straightening cushions and venetian blinds, checking the room temperature, setting out food, and otherwise attending to the needs of the people around her.

Her radiant smile illuminates a face already brightened by her dark sparkling eyes. A kind and caring woman, Dottie McNeil isn't one to check her church lady credentials at the door. No, indeed! She lives her faith and daily spreads the Good News wherever she goes.

Dottie's church, Second New Saint Paul Baptist, is serious about teaching its youngest members to be leaders, and Dottie is serious about helping to make that happen. For more than twenty-five years, the church has developed young Christians by giving them leadership roles in the Youth Church and by providing them with exceptional social, recreational, and educational opportunities. Dottie McNeil was president of the Youth Fellowship and Youth Church before recently stepping down after seven years of providing motivation, guidance, and direction to the children and parents involved.

While the adults are downstairs in the main sanctuary holding Sunday morning worship services, the children are running the Youth Church upstairs. The youth-led service follows the same order of worship and takes about the same length of time as the regular service.

Mrs. Dorothy McNeil, former President of the Youth Fellowship Committee and the Youth Church, pays rapt attention to the sermon delivered by a teenage preacher.

The big difference is that every task, from preaching to collecting the offering, is performed by young people whose congregation is made up mostly of children ranging in age from babies to teenagers. The Youth Church has its own choir, deacons, missionaries, nurses, and ushers. As they grow up, some of those who were ministers in the Youth Church leave to become pastors of their own churches. Throughout it all, the mother hen of church ladies is there to make sure everything turns out just right.

Cherry Fluff

It's a sin to tell a lie, but if you need a last-minute dessert that looks as if it took you hours to make, you should try this one.

MAKES 12 (½-CUP) SERVINGS

1 (14-ounce) can sweetened condensed milk
1 (16-ounce) container extra creamy frozen
    whipped topping, thawed
1 (20-ounce) can pineapple tidbits, well
    drained
1 (20-ounce) can cherry pie filling
½ cup chopped pecans
3 drops red food coloring (optional)

• • • Fold together the milk and whipped topping in a large bowl. Add the remaining ingredients, stirring well. Refrigerate 1 hour before serving.

—Mrs. Nuntiata Buck

Bananas Jackson

Flamboyant in presentation but deliciously simple to make, Bananas Jackson is a favorite with men.

MAKES 6 TO 8 SERVINGS

¼ cup butter or margarine
½ cup sugar
1 teaspoon lime juice
Dash of cinnamon
4 large, firm, ripe bananas, peeled and sliced
    diagonally
2 teaspoons bourbon
1 teaspoon banana liqueur

• • • Combine the butter, sugar, lime juice, and cinnamon in a 10-inch sauté pan. Cook, stirring often, until the sugar caramelizes. Stir the bananas into the caramelized mixture; cook 5 minutes, basting frequently with the sauce. Remove from the heat. Drizzle on the bourbon and banana liqueur. Serve over vanilla ice cream. (The heat cooks out the alcohol, leaving only the flavors.)

—*Ms. Nicale Portis*

. . . .

Pineapple Stuffing

This is an easy dish to whip up for supper following afternoon church programs. Delicious addition to a holiday meal, as a dessert, or as a side dish with ham or turkey.

MAKES 8 TO 10 SERVINGS

8 slices day-old white bread, shredded
1 (15-ounce) can crushed pineapple
1 cup sugar
3 large eggs, well beaten
¼ stick butter or margarine, melted
    and cooled

• • •Preheat the oven to 350°F. Grease an 11-cup casserole dish. Place the shredded bread in the greased casserole dish, then add the can of crushed pineapple, sugar, and beaten eggs. Gently stir together. Stir in the butter. Bake 45 minutes to 1 hour. Serve warm.

—*Ms. Tonya McNeal*

. . . .

Cream Puffs

When prepared correctly, the puffs are light as angels' wings and the filling is rich as sin. Quite a combination!

MAKES 16 MEDIUM-SIZE SERVINGS

1 cup water
½ cup shortening
1 cup all-purpose flour
½ teaspoon salt
4 large eggs
1 (3-ounce) package vanilla pudding,
    cooked as directed
½ (8-ounce) container frozen whipped
    topping, thawed
Powdered sugar
1 cup semisweet chocolate chips, melted

• • •Preheat the oven to 425°F. Boil the water and shortening until dissolved. Add the flour and salt all at once and cook, stirring constantly, until the mixture leaves the sides of the saucepan. Stir into ball and remove from heat. Add the eggs, one at a time, beating with an electric mixer after each addition. Drop by the tablespoon onto a greased cookie sheet. Bake at 425°F for 15 minutes, then 375°F for 20 minutes. Let cool in the oven with the door open for 20 minutes. Cool completely on a wire rack; cut in half. Cook pudding as directed on package. Pour into a medium-size bowl and cool. Fold in the half container of whipped topping. Fill pastries with pudding mixture. Place top back on, sprinkle with powdered sugar and drizzle with melted chocolate chips. Serve immediately.

NOTE: If using the next day, store shells in an airtight bag in the refrigerator and stuff before serving.

—*adapted from* Rumford Complete Cookbook

Gladly the Cross I'd Bear

MRS. DON'T-YOU-DARE-USE-MY-NAME

A certain former first lady, who refuses to give her name, tells the story of when her husband retired and a new shepherd came to lead the congregation. Her husband, a venerable and respected preacher if ever there was one, was in the habit of wearing a clerical collar and cross as part of his ecclesiastical attire. It was the tradition among pastors of his generation to do so. But the new pastor had no patience with tradition.

He was heard to remark, from the pulpit no less, that he couldn't stand seeing Methodist clergy wearing collars and crosses big enough to hang Jesus from. "Mrs. Don't-You-Dare-Use-My-Name" said her first impulse was "to get up right then, march to the front of the church, and slap him clean out of the pulpit." But, being the good Christian woman she was, she prayed hard to avoid that sin.

What she couldn't avoid was going up to him after church and telling him about himself. Before she could stop herself, she said to him, "You're going to make me lose my soul because I want to put that cross around your neck and hang you with it." She confesses, "I'm not even supposed to be thinking like that, let alone tell anyone about it. But I did."

CHAPTER 7

Beverages

*Mrs. Bessie Brazley, right, in the church parking
lot with Mrs. Carolyn Rhodes.*

Experience Counts

The Toulminville-Warren United Methodist Church, unlike Baptist and Pentecostal denominations, does not have an official designation of "Mother of the Church." If it did, Mrs. Bessie Brazley would have won the title hands down. Age, wisdom, and experience are the distinguishing characteristics of Mothers of the Church, and Mrs. Brazley had them all. Her prayerful support of the church was accompanied by her faithful service. A loyal member of her church for more years than anyone living could count, she volunteered wherever she was needed. Mrs. Brazley belonged to the Good Samaritans Club and helped prepare food for the Repast following funerals. She guided younger women in their Christian duty, and she instructed children on the correct way to behave during worship. Like women in other churches who bear the honorary title, Mrs. Brazley was an opinion leader. Her comments could make or break the career of a new pastor, and her words could cause any program to soar or sink.

Mrs. Brazley knew the story of every family in the church and was connected to many of them by blood or marriage. Her husband had the most powerful baritone in the church choir, and her brother-in-law was Sunday school superintendent. Nieces, nephews, and members of her extended family often called upon her to mediate disputes and give advice. Confidante, counselor, confessor, she was a living repository of church history.

Going to church meant getting dressed up, and Mrs. Brazley was a world-class shopper. She was on a first-name basis with boutique owners all over town, who called her first when suits and dresses they knew she would like came into their stores. She wore her favorite color combination, black and white, throughout the year, cutting an elegant figure as she sat in her regular pew at church. Favored young family members were invited to sit next to her and hold her hand throughout the service.

She was a glamorous woman even into old age. Her manicured nails, high cheekbones, big, dark eyes, and smooth café-au-lait skin never revealed her true age. When her silky black hair began to gray and thin, she simply bought stylish wigs to wear beneath her endless supply of hats. Advancing age could not diminish her unmistakable loveliness. Not only was she a fashion plate, she also had a will of steel, which might on occasion bend but never would break. The last of her generation, she liberally dispensed advice that was unfailingly accurate. Mrs. Brazley was not one to mince words, she did not suffer fools gladly, and she could always be counted on to see things clearly and call them as she saw them. If there was ever a question about the right thing to do or say, your best bet was to "ask Mrs. Brazley."

In just about every church and in nearly every family, there is at least one lady who by virtue of her wisdom and experience can call all the shots if she takes a notion to do so. People turn to her as the arbiter of taste and fashion, the guardian of propriety, and the very last word on appropriate behavior and appropriate attire for weddings, christenings, funerals, and other major life events celebrated in the church. Mrs. Brazley was such a one. She upheld the standards of decency and good behavior with Statue of Liberty–like steadfastness.

Anyone who had a question about exactly how much lace was enough, or how much exposed skin was too much, could ask Mrs. Brazley and get a clear, well-reasoned answer. Her disapproval could be withering, not because of any malice in her heart, but because her pronouncements were accepted as Gospel truth. You ignored her advice at your peril.

Who knows whether the following story is true or not? It has become the stuff of family legend. They say it happened at the funeral of one of her sisters. A niece, the daughter of her departed sister, perhaps bewildered by sorrow, perhaps not knowing any better, appeared at the funeral of her mother wearing a blue plaid dress. The family only wore funereal black or resurrection white to such services. Graveside, following the burial, another relative turned to the woman and said, "If you didn't have anything to wear to your mother's funeral, you should have told me." Mrs. Brazley rushed to the woman's defense and said, "She wore exactly what her mother would have wanted her to wear." Like many of her pronouncements, this comment revealed her tender heart. It was a truly caring thing to say at a painful moment. Mrs. Brazley was one of the most loving and Christian women I have ever known, though she could scare the taste out of your mouth if you made her angry.

She prayed for her family members constantly and struggled to accept God's will, no matter how unfathomable it might have been. She appreciated the symbolism of clothing and lived by the rule that what showed on the outside reflected what was on the inside. Whether one agreed or disagreed with her point of view, there was never any doubt she believed that there was a right way and a wrong way to do things, and there are times when doing the right thing is the only thing to do.

While her standards were high and hard to meet, she never asked anyone to do anything she was not willing to do herself.

Church Supper Iced Tea

Regardless of the season, what would a church supper be without fresh brewed iced tea?

MAKES 30 (8-OUNCE) SERVINGS

22 to 25 tea bags
2 cups sugar
2 cups pineapple juice
2 cups orange juice with pulp
2 oranges, thinly sliced
1 lemon, thinly sliced
1 bunch fresh mint

• • • Boil 1½ gallons water in a large saucepan. Remove from the heat. Add the tea bags. Cover and steep until the water is the color of coffee. Remove the tea bags. Stir in the sugar until it dissolves. Add the juices. Taste and adjust for sweetness, if needed. Serve over crushed ice garnished with fruit slices and mint.

—Brenda Rhodes Miller

Bible School Punch

Messy and sticky and oh-so-sweet, this punch has been a favorite of Vacation Bible scholars for generations.

MAKES 3 QUARTS OR 16 (6-OUNCE) SERVINGS

1 (11.5-ounce) can Hawaiian Punch
    concentrate
1 (12-ounce) can frozen lemonade
12 ounces orange juice
Sugar to taste
1 (2-liter) bottle 7 UP

• • • Mix all the ingredients in a large bowl. Serve over crushed ice.

—Ms. Vyllorya A. Evans

Doing Things Nobody Else Will Do

MRS. DORETHA MANUEL
Bethlehem Baptist Church
Citronelle, Alabama

The title Sunday School Superintendent sounds like an exalted position. But, as Mrs. Doretha Manuel will tell anyone who asks, it is really a job that means doing what nobody else wants to do. She manages the Sunday school program, makes sure it starts and stops on time, goes over lessons, fills in when teachers are absent, checks the library, and she handles Vacation Bible School. Basically, her job is to run the Christian education program of her church.

First lady Mrs. Lolita Cusic, left, toasts Sunday School Superintendent Doretha Manuel with a glass of ginger punch.

She especially enjoys previewing videos to use in Sunday school. "We have videos on the Old Testament and the New Testament books that I check to see if they are compatible with our Sunday school lessons. Right now, the children are glued to the *Miracles of Jesus* tape. That video follows Scripture very well and works perfectly with our lesson."

In real life, she is a hairdresser who credits the Holy Spirit with guiding her work. "I wrote our Vacation Bible School curriculum. We aimed for teaching salvation, and with the help of the Holy Spirit, somehow we got there."

A member of the church choir who makes a joyful noise with the other sopranos, Mrs. Manuel also plays violin with a string group that recently produced a CD. Each Sunday, she takes her three children to church where they are active members of the faith community, just like their mother.

Ginger Punch

It's the ginger that makes this punch special and gives it a non-alcoholic kick.

MAKES ABOUT 24 (8-OUNCE) SERVINGS

2 (5-inch) pieces fresh gingerroot
3 cups sugar
2 cups water
1 gallon cranberry-raspberry juice
1 (46-ounce) can pineapple juice
1 quart ginger beer or strong ginger ale

• • • Peel and finely grate the gingerroot pieces. Place the grated gingerroot and the sugar in a medium saucepan with the 2 cups water. Bring to a boil, stirring constantly. Boil for 5 minutes or until a syrup forms. Mash the gingerroot well and then strain. Place the strained syrup in a large punch bowl. Add the cranberry-raspberry juice and pineapple juice. Add ginger beer or strong ginger ale just before serving; mix well. If desired, serve over an ice ring made of cranberry-raspberry juice. To make an ice ring, freeze juice in a round plastic container. Dip in hot water to unmold.

—Ms. Dora Finley

Emergency Punch

An old-time Communion steward offered this recipe as a way to use up opened bottles of grape juice that might not "keep" until the next first Sunday.

MAKES 5 SERVINGS

1 quart grape juice
Juice of four large lemons
Sugar to taste
1 (8-ounce) bottle 7 UP

• • • Mix juices and sugar in a round glass pitcher. Fill with 7 UP and stir well. Serve over ice in tall glasses.

—Mrs. Lottie T. Rhodes

Frappe

It's fun to coordinate sherbet color with colors for a bridal or baby shower. Frappe is almost a requirement at church teas.

MAKES ABOUT 20 (8-OUNCE) SERVINGS

1 gallon ginger ale
1 quart fruit sherbet

• • • Pour ginger ale over blocks of fruit sherbet in a large punch bowl. Serve in punch cups.

—Mrs. Bessie Brazley

Holiday Punch

The bright color and sparkling taste make this a favorite punch for church events from Thanksgiving through the New Year.

MAKES 1½ GALLONS

1 gallon cranberry juice cocktail
1 quart orange juice
1 (12-ounce) can lemon-lime soda
1 (1-liter) bottle ginger ale
1 cup sugar

• • • Combine all the ingredients in a large punch bowl, stirring well. Fill the bowl with crushed ice. Serve immediately.

—*Ms. Vyllorya A. Evans*

Pineapple Ginger Punch

When the theme of the church tea is "Caribbean Carnival," serve this punch with Tropical Ice Box Fruit Cake for a real taste of the Islands.

MAKES ABOUT 24 (8-OUNCE) SERVINGS

2 (46-ounce) cans pineapple juice
3 quarts ginger beer or strong ginger ale
2 cups canned pineapple cubes (drained)

• • • Combine all the ingredients in a large bowl. Mix well before serving.

—*Mrs. Doretha Manuel*

Won't Stain Punch

This is the punch to serve to children, because it won't leave stains on their Sunday clothes.

MAKES 18 TO 20 SERVINGS

3 lemon wedges
1 cup sugar
1 (12-ounce) can frozen lemonade
1 (64-ounce) can pineapple juice
1 (1-liter) bottle ginger ale
½ gallon pineapple sherbet (optional)
Maraschino cherries (garnish)
Sprigs of fresh mint (garnish)

• • • Wipe the rim of a large punch bowl with the lemon wedges. Spread the sugar on a cookie sheet. Dip the punch bowl into the sugar, making a frosted rim around the edge of the bowl. Pour the lemonade concentrate, pineapple juice, and ginger ale into the punch bowl; mix well. Fill the punch bowl with finely crushed ice or pineapple sherbet if you prefer. Serve garnished with cherries and sprigs of fresh mint.

—*Mrs. Melanie Shelwood*

Fruit Punch

This punch is almost a dessert in itself. Serve very cold.

MAKES 20 (8-OUNCE) SERVINGS

1 (3-ounce) package lime gelatin
2 cups hot water
2 cups sugar
2 cups cold water
1 (46-ounce) can pineapple juice
1 (8-ounce) bottle lemon juice
1 (1-ounce) bottle almond flavoring
1 quart or 2 liters chilled ginger ale
½ gallon orange sherbet (optional)

• • • Combine the gelatin, hot water, and sugar in a large container. Stir until the gelatin and sugar are dissolved. Add the cold water, pineapple juice, lemon juice, and almond flavoring; mix well. When ready to serve, add the chilled ginger ale; mix well. Serve in punch bowl over ice or over orange sherbet, if desired.

—Mrs. Juanita Eaton

Mint Tea

A "must have" for Harvest Teas, Mint Tea is a popular beverage for adults.

MAKES 4 SERVINGS

3 tea bags
4 cups boiling water
½ cup crushed mint leaves
5 tablespoons sugar
Mint sprigs for garnish

• • • Add the tea bags to the boiling water in a saucepan. Stir in the crushed mint leaves. Cover and steep for 5 minutes. Remove the tea bags and the mint leaves and stir in the sugar. Serve hot or cold garnished with mint sprigs.

—Ms. Joyce Fourth

Ginger Tea

Brew this refreshing beverage to warm up choir members' voices. It is also good for colds and cramps.

MAKES 4 TO 6 SERVINGS

1 (1-inch-long) piece fresh gingerroot or ¼ to ½
    teaspoon ground ginger
3 tea bags
4 cups boiling water
Pinch of salt
6 teaspoons sugar or to taste

• • • Place the gingerroot between two pieces of waxed paper. Pound with a mallet until finely ground. Add the tea bags to the boiling water in a saucepan. Stir in the ground ginger.

Cover and steep for 5 minutes; remove the tea bags. Stir in the sugar and serve hot or iced.

—Ms. Joyce Felder

. . . .

Russian Tea

The other "must have" beverage for Harvest Teas, this is especially good served hot.

MAKES 8 SERVINGS

1 (4-inch) piece cinnamon stick
1½ teaspoons whole cloves
2 tablespoons loose black tea
¼ cup honey
½ cup sugar
1 cup water
Grated rind of 1 orange
6 cups boiling water
⅔ cup orange juice
¼ cup lemon juice
1 seedless orange, sliced

• • •Simmer the cinnamon stick, cloves, black tea, honey, sugar, and 1 cup water in a large saucepan for 10 minutes. Remove from the heat; cover and let steep for 1 hour. Add the grated rind; steep for 1 minute; strain. Stir in the boiling water, juices, and orange slices. Serve hot or cold. Remove the orange slices if storing any remaining tea overnight.

—Mrs. Melanie Shelwood

. . . .

Country Lemonade

Lemonade mixes are no match for the taste of fresh, homemade Country Lemonade. Press little helpers into service squeezing plenty of juice for the next pitcher . . . and the next.

MAKES 6 TO 8 SERVINGS

1 cup hot water
1½ cups sugar
⅛ teaspoon salt
1 quart cold water
Juice of 6 large lemons (⅔ cup lemon juice)
2 lemons for slices and rind
Sugar for dipping

• • •Combine the hot water, 1½ cups sugar, and salt in a large container. Stir until the sugar dissolves. Add the cold water and the lemon juice. Mix well. Taste for sweetness, adding more sugar if needed. Serve with thin slices of lemon floating in each glass. To frost the rim of the glass, rub the rim with the lemon rind and then dip in sugar.

—Brenda Rhodes Miller

. . . .

Aunt Shorty's Pastor Meets B.B. King

MAE BELLE POLK
Pilgrim Rest Baptist Church
El Campo, Texas

Mae Belle got her nickname, Shorty, because she was barely five feet tall in her highest-heeled shoes, the ones she saved for dancing. Everybody in the family was taller than she was, so they all called her Shorty. A lifetime member of Piggy Rest, which is how people affectionately referred to Pilgrim Rest Baptist Church, Shorty sang in the choir in her early years. Later on, she was in Missionary Circle # 2, drawing on her legendary cooking skills to minister to the sick and shut-in.

In the 1950s, B.B. King waxed his first record, "Three O'Clock in the Morning." and Christmas Eve that same year, he came to El Campo to play at Son Taylor's Tip Top Inn. Shorty was there in her high-heeled dancing shoes, along with just about everybody else in town, church ladies included.

Miss Mae Belle Polk, also known as Shorty, poses in front of a stained glass window in her church.

That night the club was packed with people laughing and drinking and dancing. It was party time for real, and nobody was going home before B.B. sang his new hit song. The closer it got to closing time, the noisier and more excited the crowd became. All of a sudden, a hush fell over the entire club. Everybody looked around to see what had caused the silence. And there stood the pastor of Shorty's church, not saying a word, not frowning, not smiling, just watching. His gaze took in the tables littered with beer bottles and the couples dancing cheek to cheek.

"Three O'Clock in the Morning" was the last song played that night, and as soon as B.B. and Lucille, his guitar, hit that final chord, people dashed out of the place as if they were escaping a fire. They walked as fast as they could past the pastor, trying their best to be invisible. He still hadn't said a mumbling word.

Christmas day, there was a sunrise service at five o'clock in the morning. Footsore and weary, those members of Pilgrim Rest who had closed Son Taylor's arrived at church expecting the worst.

Once again, the pastor just stood in the doorway, not saying a word. As the dancers and club patrons appeared, he pointed them one and all in the direction of the mourners' bench up in front of the entire church. Each person, including Shorty, was made to stand up and apologize for being at the dance, even though not one of them was really sorry he or she had gone.

Banana-Peach Milk Shake

MAKES 2 SERVINGS

1 cup ice
2 peaches, peeled and sliced
½ banana
1 cup milk
1 tablespoon malted milk
1 tablespoon sugar

• • • Partially chop the ice in a blender. Add the peaches, banana, milk, malted milk, and sugar. Blend until the desired thickness.

—Philonese Thompson

Jammin' Rum Punch

MAKES ABOUT 1½ GALLONS

1 (46-ounce) can unsweetened pineapple
  juice
½ gallon plus 2 cups orange juice
1 (1-liter) bottle dark rum
½ cup grenadine or cherry syrup

• • • Combine all the ingredients in a large container; mix well. Chill. Pour into glasses filled with ice cubes.

NOTE: Garnish with maraschino cherries, fresh pineapple, and orange twists on decorative picks.

—Mary Ellen Robinson

CHAPTER 8

Top It Off:
Sauces, Frosting,
Fillings, and
Glazes

*The First Couple of the Free Gospel Deliverance
Temple in Coral Hills, Maryland—
Pastor and First Lady Green.*

But the Woman Is the Glory of the Man

Many African-American churches confer the title First Lady on the pastor's wife. When and how this practice originated is unclear, but at the very least, the First Lady of an African-American Protestant Church is generally spoken of in a tone of voice that implies the use of her title in capital letters.

The First Lady may have her own special pew, and in large churches she may actually have a suite of offices dedicated to her use. Churches celebrate the First Lady's birthday and they hold First Lady teas. There are even vendors at annual church conventions hawking everything from jewelry to panty hose emblazoned with the title.

Despite all the hullabaloo, there is no secret to how you acquire the position—simply by virtue of being married to the pastor. There is only one First Lady per church. The widows of deceased or retired pastors are often accorded special respect, but that's another story. Assistant and associate ministers may well have wives, and with the growing number of women clergy, they may also have husbands, but those spouses have no special title or designation. Only the pastor's wife is called FIRST LADY.

Being First Lady is no easy task. The position requires advanced diplomatic and organizational skills. In other words, it can involve a great deal of biting one's tongue. Depending on the congregation, demands made upon the First Lady can be extraordinary. In some churches, she attends every single worship service, every funeral, and every wedding. Wherever her husband goes in his official capacity, she is expected to be at his side.

She might be so much a part of his ministry that she even sits in the pulpit with him, taking her turn at preaching the Gospel. Or, she might simply take her seat in a pew, always the same one, always in the same place, shouting or smiling, depending on what he requires and needs. She often takes a tremendously active role, becoming involved in multiple projects, highly visible, with her own followers and fans. She might direct the choir or be a church musician. She is generally a fixture of the Sunday school, the youth group, or the women's ministry. Although she may have many talents, she may decide to be simply her husband's silent partner, never taking a stand and never attracting undue attention to herself. She might be a fashion plate, setting the standard for other women in the church, or she might care nothing for clothes.

First Ladies, like all church ladies, come in all shapes and sizes, all temperaments and ages, all kinds of personalities, all styles of being, and nearly every faith and denomination. To identify the really serious ones, look for the hats. In the old days, every woman and every girl wore a hat to church. It wasn't a matter of choice; it was simply an expected part of their appropriate attire.

First Lady Mrs. Lucy Hall and Pastor Shelvin Hall welcoming guests to Friendship Baptist Church.

Then, a wave of hatlessness swept the country, and only a few old souls, mostly mothers of the church, clung to their hats, until gradually, the joy of hat wearing returned to the land.

Today, we are in the midst of a hat renaissance, with hat shops springing up in every mall and on many downtown streets. Millinery shops are once more in vogue, and department stores are restoring hat departments left and right. The *Essence* catalog even offers elegant and elaborate hats through the mail.

But wiser souls than I have noted that First Ladies must do much more than simply look the part. It is an unspoken fact that the pastor and his wife are the "parents" of the church. They set the tone for how men and women of their congregation behave among themselves, and, whatever their private relationship, in the context of the church, the pastor and the First Lady must act as if they're on the same team. They must be harmonious, supportive, loving, and in "one accord." Nothing sets church tongues wagging faster than a whiff of discord between the pastor and his wife. A married couple at the head of the church who don't get along could actually mean the demise of the church. So being a First Lady is no joke. Outspoken women probably have the hardest time of it. They have to find a way to balance their personal need for autonomy with their desire to be their husband's helpmeet. There are even support groups for First Ladies, in which experienced and successful members of this exclusive club share their secrets with other wives.

New wives who are also new First Ladies face the twofold challenge of learning how to function in a marriage while also learning how to function in a church. It can be a daunting prospect. Women who marry before their husbands are called to preach may struggle as their spouses strive to do God's will, becoming First Ladies only after the call is accepted. Still others may marry a new or established pastor, carving out their own place in his ministry. Indeed, some First Ladies discover that they themselves are called and become co-pastors with their husbands.

And finally, there are First Ladies like me. When I married a Baptist preacher and pastor, one question I heard all the time was "How does it feel to be First Lady?"

What could I say? I love my husband. His calling is his own. I tell anyone who will listen that I married the man, not the pastor. I signed up to be his wife; I didn't sign up to be First Lady.

Not that anyone ever pays the slightest bit of attention to my declaration. If you're married to the pastor of a church, like it or not, you are First Lady. It depends on you whether that title is written in capital letters or not.

Fruit Sauce

This topping sends plain pound cake to celestial heights!

MAKES 8 TO 10 SERVINGS

½ cup each of strawberries, honeydew cubes,
    blueberries, raspberries, pineapple chunks
    (if canned, well drained), and banana
    slices
1 cup orange juice
½ teaspoon finely ground ginger
½ cup crushed mint leaves

• • • Combine the fruit and orange juice in a large bowl. Toss together with the ginger and mint. Serve over pound cake and Lemon Mountains (page 45), if desired.

—*Brenda Rhodes Miller*

Creamy Vanilla Sauce

Here's one time when plain vanilla is no joke. This delicious sauce adds a special flavor to chocolate cake and to almost any pudding.

MAKES 1⅓ CUPS

¼ cup sugar
⅛ teaspoon salt
1 teaspoon all-purpose flour

1 large egg, beaten
1 cup light cream
1 teaspoon vanilla

• • • Combine the sugar, salt, and flour in a small saucepan; add the egg, mixing well. Gradually stir in the cream. Cook over medium heat, stirring constantly until mixture thickens and coats a spoon. Remove from the heat and stir in the vanilla. Serve over chocolate pound cake.

—*adapted from* Edith Barber's Cookbook

Grape Sauce

The same communion steward who makes the grape juice punch makes this grape sauce as a way to use up the half bottle of grape juice left each Sunday. Waste not, want not.

MAKES 8 TO 10 SERVINGS

1¼ cups sugar
1 cup water
½ cup light or dark grape juice
Juice of 1 lemon (about 3 tablespoons)

• • • Combine the sugar and water in a medium saucepan. Bring to a boil while stirring constantly; cook about 5 minutes or until a thick syrup forms. Remove from the heat and cool. Stir in the grape and lemon juices, mixing well. Refrigerate to allow the sauce to thicken before serving. Serve over fresh fruit, peanut butter ice cream, or angel food cake topped with ice cream.

—*adapted from* **Rumford Complete Cookbook**

. . . .

Maple Sauce

Maple syrup fans will definitely enjoy this topping, while corn and cane syrup fans may take a bit of convincing.

MAKES 2 CUPS

2 large egg yolks, well beaten
⅔ cup warm maple syrup
Pinch of salt
1 cup whipping cream, whipped

• • • Place the beaten yolks in the top of a double boiler. Pour the warm syrup slowly over them while stirring. Cook over medium heat, while continuing to stir, until the consistency of thin custard. Remove from the heat and cool. Stir in the salt and fold in the whipped cream. Serve immediately over fresh berries, poached pears, baked apples, Belgian waffles, rice pudding, angel food cake, ice cream, or a dessert of your choice.

—*adapted from* **Rumford Complete Cookbook**

. . . .

Butter Frosting

An easy no-cook frosting for your favorite cake. Extra good for the Family and Friends meal at church.

MAKES 1½ CUPS

1 (16-ounce) package powdered sugar
½ cup butter
½ teaspoon salt
1 teaspoon vanilla
1 tablespoon (or more) milk

• • • Sift the sugar into a medium bowl. Add the butter, creaming together until well blended. Stir in the salt, vanilla, and 1 tablespoon milk, mixing well. Add extra milk if needed for spreading consistency. Spread over the cooled cake.

—*adapted from* **Anyone Can Bake**

. . . .

Whipped Butter Frosting

The head of the Hospitality Committee swears by this cooked frosting, which is almost like a "hard sauce" and good for cake or fruit puddings.

MAKES ENOUGH TO FROST A 2-LAYER CAKE

4½ tablespoons all-purpose flour
1½ cups milk
1½ cups butter
1½ cups sugar
1½ teaspoons bourbon
1 teaspoon vanilla flavoring

• • • Make a paste of flour and a small portion of the milk in a medium saucepan. Use a wire whisk to stir the mixture while adding the remaining milk. Cook over low heat until thick, stirring or whisking constantly; cool. Cream the butter, sugar, bourbon, and vanilla in a medium bowl until fluffy. Add the cooled mixture and beat until the consistency of whipped cream. (Do not overbeat or mixture will separate.) Spread between layers and over sides and top of a layer cake.

—Mary Ellen Robinson

. . . .

Brown Sugar Frosting

Perfect frosting for nutty cakes.

MAKES 2 CUPS

1 stick butter or margarine
1 cup packed light brown sugar
¼ cup milk
1¾ cups powdered sugar
1 teaspoon vanilla

• • • Combine the butter and brown sugar in a medium saucepan. Cook over medium heat, stirring constantly, until boiling. Boil 2 minutes. Add the milk; boil 3 minutes. Sift in the powdered sugar and beat until smooth with an electric mixer. Add the vanilla. Add small amounts of cold water if needed for consistency. Use to frost spice or chocolate cake.

—Mrs. Gracie Briggs

. . . .

Pineapple Cream Cheese Frosting

This is a very sweet, smooth frosting, best on a plain cake that's not too sweet. You can substitute any fruit-flavored cream cheese.

MAKES ENOUGH FROSTING FOR ONE
BUNDT CAKE

1 (8-ounce) container pineapple cream cheese
2 cups powdered sugar
1 teaspoon vanilla
1–3 tablespoons cream or milk

• • • Combine the cream cheese and powdered sugar in a medium bowl; beat well. Stir in the vanilla and enough cream to make the frosting spread easily; mix well.

—Mrs. Lolita Cusic

. . . .

The Pastor's Helpmeet

Craig Memorial Community Church
Adelphi, Maryland

She makes the role of First Lady seem virtually effortless. Despite an impossibly busy schedule, Mrs. Brenda Swanson is totally unflappable. She exemplifies the perfect blend of enthusiasm, organizational genius, patience, and compassion. Her unique abilities make her the ideal helpmeet for her husband, the Pastor of Craig Memorial Community Church, Rev. Claude Swanson.

Craig Memorial has an active music ministry and five choirs—the senior choir, a men's choir, the children's choir, Instruments of Praise, which is a choir made up of young adult women, and a Gospel choir. The leadership of the music ministry is composed of the presidents of all the choirs along with seven other members and Mrs. Swanson.

She not only helps to plan the ministry's activities but also coordinates the scheduling of choirs to accompany the pastor to outside preaching engagements and assigns musicians to every service held at the church. Because music is such an important part of the worship experience, she is also involved in developing a budget for the music ministry and in administering the salaries of all the musicians.

In addition to her work with the music ministry, Mrs. Swanson also fills in as chair of the Culinary Committee. This group is responsible for preparing food for all activities held at church, including those sponsored by groups renting the church's facility for banquets or receptions. The Culinary Committee works hand in hand with the Facilities Committee and the Hospitality Committee. Facilities is charged with setting up tables and chairs, placing audiovisual equipment, and generally making sure the rooms are ready for use. Hospitality decorates the dining hall for special events, and its members slice cakes, mix punch, put out the food prepared by Culinary, and make sure all guests are taken care of and made to feel welcome.

Somehow in her jam-packed schedule she found time to put on a fashion show at the church called *Hats of Praise*. "I didn't want to charge admission to the hat fashion show. Instead, I put together a pretty basket of party foods, including a ham, gourmet jellies, crackers, and other treats. We made an announcement that if anyone wanted to make a donation toward the cost of the basket to go ahead and we'd accept it. We couldn't run a raffle at church, but you could win the basket by making a contribution and giving your name. It really went over well!"

Top It Off   177

Holy Madame Brown

MRS. LOLITA CUSIC
New Life Christian Ministries of Greater Chicago
Chicago, Illinois

Holy Madame Brown had the faith of a child. As a little girl, she spent six days of the week immersed in Bible verses, hymns, and everything holy. Her real name was Lolita, but her big sisters used to tease her, and they nicknamed her Holy Madame Brown, which was the name of a popular radio evangelist at the time. They poked fun at her, calling her a fool for her pious ways and her penchant for quoting Scripture, especially "He who calls his brother a fool will burn in the pits of hell forever."

Yet Scripture meant something to that little girl, who trusted her God as only a little child can. She believed He heard her prayers, like the one she prayed at the bedside of her beloved Aunt Honey.

In the 1970s Madame Brown went to Faith Lutheran, a sweet little school where religion was as much a part of the curriculum as math or history. For years, she could name all the books of the Bible without missing a beat.

At Christmas, the little school put on a play, with everyone from the tiny kindergarten students to the oh-so-worldly sixth graders participating. One year, they marched in holding candles, joyously singing "Bring a Torch, Jeanette Isabella." Everyone's family turned out, knowing the children had worked hard to learn their pieces. They overlooked any little glitches, such as the time one of the kids dropped the baby Jesus.

Faith Lutheran was also where Madame Brown and some of the other little girls first flexed their feminist muscles. The whole school went to chapel every Friday, where they would sing and listen to the pastor. At some point

From left to right, first ladies Mrs. Lolita Cusic and Mrs. Della Russell share a smile with Sunday school class leader Mrs. Bessie Samples.

Madame Brown noticed there weren't any girls involved in the service. Boys collected the offering, and a boy served as the acolyte. Somehow, it didn't seem fair. So Madame Brown and her crew talked to the pastor about it. He listened to their concerns, and thereafter, girls got to collect the offering, although they still weren't allowed to be acolytes.

If Faith Lutheran was where Madame Brown spent her weekdays, on Sundays she was in Sunday school at a United Methodist Church. Thanks to both her churches, Madame Brown grew up singing hymns and cantatas, reciting Easter and Christmas speeches, and learning to be a Christian.

Today, Madame Brown is a pastor's wife and a mother who goes to church every single Sunday. These days, she's the one working with trusting children on their Christmas and Easter plays. The church is a big part of who she was, is, and will be. These days, the memory of her sisters' teasing doesn't hurt her feelings. She's come to realize there's nothing wrong with being Holy Madame Brown. Amen.

Lemon Frosting

Crown your gingerbread with this luscious and lemony topping, and it will be fit for a King or the Queen of the May.

MAKES ABOUT 2 CUPS

Juice of 4 lemons (about 12 tablespoons)
About 4½ cups powdered sugar, finely sifted

• • • Strain the lemon juice into a medium bowl. Add the sugar, a little at a time, until reaching a consistency that's spreadable. Spread over the cake and smooth with a thin-bladed knife that has been dipped in water. Use as a topping on loaf or breakfast breads.

—*Ms. Beverly Crandall*

Orange Frosting

Use this fabulous frosting to turn even your simplest cake-mix cake into something very special for a church event.

MAKES ABOUT 2 CUPS

1¾ cups sugar
⅓ cup cold water
3 large egg yolks
½ teaspoon grated orange zest
2 teaspoons orange juice

• • • Boil the sugar and water in a medium saucepan. Stir until the sugar dissolves partially, then boil without stirring until syrup spins 6-inch threads. Beat the egg yolks in a medium bowl; stir in the orange zest. Slowly pour the hot syrup over the yolks, stirring con-

Parting the Waters?

REVEREND CLARENCE EARL MILLER
Friendship Baptist Church
Chicago, Illinois

Rev. Clarence Earl Miller, also known as Too Tee Waters, grew up in El Campo, Texas, where just about every other Black person belonged to one of the five churches in town: the African Methodist Episcopal Church, the United Methodist Church, or one of the three Baptist churches. Pilgrim Rest was Rev. Miller's church.

During Rev. Miller's boyhood, there were only three professions in El Campo—preacher, teacher, and nurse. Everybody else who had a job worked in rice, cotton, or cattle. The rice field was a wet and messy place to earn a living. Picking cotton was hard, backbreaking labor, and both the rice mills and the cotton mills drained the life from men and women alike. Herding cattle was dirty, dusty work. The slaughterhouses, filled with terrified, bellowing animals and bloody carcasses, could put one off meat for a lifetime.

Manual labor required sturdy, durable clothing all week long. But once every week church folks put aside their battered sun hats, faded smocks, and denim coveralls to dress in their Sunday-go-to-meeting clothes. Then they could walk proudly to church and praise the Lord.

Rev. Miller paints a picture of the El Campo church ladies on their way to Pilgrim Rest. "An old rickety wooden footbridge led to the church grounds. Often as not, water was knee-deep over that bridge. I can still see the ladies getting ready to cross, their neatly braided hair covered with mail-order hats, their print dresses topped with lacy shawls. On their side of the bridge, all the ladies paused to take off their shoes and stockings, hitch up their skirts, and cross in an orderly line to the other side."

Once they got on dry land, the ladies would rush like a gaggle of geese into the church. As

Young church ladies outside Pilgrim Rest Baptist Church, El Campo, Texas, in the early 1950s.

Rev. Miller says, "In the vestibule the ladies would collapse on wooden benches for a minute before rummaging in their bags for towels to dry their feet. Getting a second wind, they'd hold their shawls up to make modesty curtains for one another as they hurriedly pulled on their stockings and wriggled into their shoes." Decently dressed again for Sunday service, the church ladies could walk with dignity to their seats and bow their heads in thanksgiving for another day of worship.

stantly. When it begins to thicken, stir in the orange juice. Cool before frosting the cake.

—*adapted from* Anyone Can Bake

. . . .

Chocolate Frosting

Sunday school cupcakes with chocolate frosting are big favorites for children and parents!

MAKES ABOUT 2 CUPS

1 (3-ounce) package cream cheese
1 tablespoon milk
1 teaspoon vanilla
Pinch of salt
2½ cups powdered sugar
½ stick butter or margarine, softened
1 (1-ounce) square sweet chocolate, melted

• • • Combine all the ingredients in a large bowl; mix well. Add additional powdered sugar if needed to achieve spreading consistency.

——*Ms. Joyce Felder*

. . . .

Cocoa Frosting

Visiting congregations will remember your cake when you cover it with this spectacular frosting.

ABOUT 2 CUPS

3 cups sugar
⅔ cup unsweetened cocoa powder
⅛ teaspoon salt
1½ cups evaporated milk
½ stick butter or margarine
1 teaspoon vanilla
½ cup finely chopped pecans

• • • Combine the sugar, cocoa, and salt in a large saucepan; mix well. Add the milk and bring to a boil over medium heat, stirring often. Add the butter; boil, while stirring, until a small amount of mixture dropped in cold water forms a ball. Remove from the heat. Stir in the vanilla. Beat until thickened. Stir in the pecans. Spread frosting over a cooled cake.

——*Ms. Joyce Felder*

. . . .

Done Paid My Vow to the Lord

SISTER MARY CONSILIO WILSON

It was late July, and she was a patient at St. Agnes Hospital in Baltimore when last I spoke with Sister Consilio. Hot afternoon sun poured into the room to light her tired, old face and bathe me in perspiration. The air conditioning was on the fritz but Sister never complained about the greenhouse temperature of her room. Indeed, she seemd as unfazed by the heat as she was delighted by my visit. An Oblate Sister of Providence for more than sixty years, Sister Consilio was no stranger to discomfort. She laughed as she told me that air conditioning was still new to her, so its absence was no real hardship.

I knew her indomitable spirit well from the days when she had been principal of the little parish grade school I attended many years ago. That spirit and her tremendous organizing ability set her apart, although each of the other nuns at St. Joseph had her own gifts.

Among her many innovations at our school, Sister Consilio had instituted the practice of playing classical music during many of the classes. We listened to opera as we worked on art projects, to Bach during arithmetic, and Handel during our science lessons. The beautiful music had a remarkable effect, helping to open our minds and allowing us to learn two things at once.

Sister was fond of playing show tunes at other times. The music served as a calming factor in classrooms crowded with energetic children. It also taught us to sing and to learn thousands of lyrics.

Sister Consilio also loved putting on musicals and festivals with elaborate dance segments. We learned the minuet, the tango, and the waltz under her direction. At her programs at Christmas, Easter, and May Day, the children recited poems, sang, and danced to the delight of their parents and friends. We never missed a step or a line, so well rehearsed and so anxious were we to please.

It was Sister Consilio who began serving hot lunches for children in the winter, recruiting parents to prepare vats of spaghetti and meatballs, chicken pot pies, tuna casseroles, and other warming dishes, which we ate in the old parish hall.

When I was a child, the sisters visited the homes of their students to share a meal with our families. It was both an honor and a daunting experience when the nuns came to dinner. Their high expectations for us made us eager to measure up to their standards.

Sister kept in touch with many of her former students and their parents, writing long letters filled with advice, information, and news clippings. Not only was she a font of wisdom when it came to education; she was also a source of advice to students when we married. I never knew what she said to the boys, but she had all sorts of tips for girls on how to be good wives and mothers, though she herself had long ago rejected marriage in favor of the religious life.

She was generous in sharing her recipes with us, admonishing us always to prepare home-cooked meals so our husbands would have a reason to come home at night. She never tired of telling us to be good listeners and to flatter our husbands' egos so they could go out and face the world with confidence. But she was quite clear that this was a two-way street: our husbands should cherish and care for us in return. She had a fine sense of the difficulty African-American families faced and did all she could to help us build strong families.

During her sixty years as an Oblate Sister of Providence, Sister Mary Consilio Wilson taught generations of boys and girls all over the country.

That late July day in St. Agnes Hospital, I had promised Sister Consilio that I would see her the next week, fully expecting that she would be released from the hospital in time for the annual Homecoming Celebration held the first Sunday in August. Sunday rolled around and I drove over to Baltimore for Mass. When I got to church, I asked the nuns standing by the door where I could find Sister Consilio. They looked at me blankly. I asked again, careful to speak clearly and with respect. The younger of the two said to me, "Sister Consilio died this morning."

I was too shocked to speak, so I sat down on the steps of the church and cried. Not for Sister Consilio. She was finally with the God she had loved so deeply all her life. I cried for my own loss.

One of the nuns handed me a tissue and shot me a look. It spoke volumes. I remembered how hard Sister Consilio had worked with me when I was a child to help me control my ever-ready tears. She hated for people to make a fuss. Wanting to honor her by behaving the way I knew she would expect of me, I wiped my eyes and went in to Mass.

Coffee Frosting

Chocolate cake with Coffee Frosting is the best of both worlds. Make it once for the Ladies' Auxiliary meeting and you'll be on the Refreshments Committee forever.

MAKES 1½ CUPS (ENOUGH FOR 12 CUPCAKES OR ONE 9-INCH CAKE)

1 cup butter or margarine
2 cups sugar
½ cup strong coffee
½ cup milk
4½ cups powdered sugar

• • • Melt the butter in a medium to large saucepan. Add the sugar; bring to a boil over low heat, stirring constantly. Boil for 4 minutes. Combine the coffee and milk; add to the sugar mixture, stirring until the mixture boils. Remove from the heat and cool. Slowly add the powdered sugar, beating with a spoon until the mixture is thick enough to spread.

—Brenda Rhodes Miller

Caramel Frosting

Candy-flavored frosting like this is so good some folks won't want to eat the cake.

MAKES 1½ CUPS

1½ cups packed light brown sugar
¾ cup thin cream or milk
1 tablespoon butter
1 teaspoon vanilla

• • • Combine the sugar, cream, and butter in a medium saucepan. Cook gently until a small amount dropped in cold water forms a soft ball. Remove saucepan from the heat; cool. Stir in the vanilla. Beat the mixture until it is thick enough to spread.

—adapted from Anyone Can Bake

Tangerine Filling

Cakes made for the Repast will be better with this great filling or glaze for pound cake.

MAKES 1⅓ CUP

1 cup sugar
4 tablespoons cornstarch
½ teaspoon salt
1 cup tangerine juice
2 tablespoons tangerine zest
1½ tablespoons lemon juice
2 tablespoons butter or margarine

• • • Combine all the ingredients in a large saucepan. Bring to a boil over high heat; boil for 1 minute, stirring constantly. Chill before using.

—*Ms. Beverly Crandall*

Lemon Glaze

Lemon Glaze is easy to make and gives a special flavor to "store-bought" pound cake, especially if you slice the cake first and then pour on the glaze.

MAKES ABOUT 1 CUP

1 cup powdered sugar
1 tablespoon lemon juice
2 tablespoons milk
1 teaspoon vegetable oil

• • • Combine the ingredients in a small bowl. Microwave on High for 20 seconds. Drizzle over cake.

—*Mrs. Carol Preston*

THE CONTRIBUTORS

Deloris Agee
Rena Agee
Dorothy Andrews
Shirlene Archer
Willette Bailey
Lucille Battle
Dr. Wiley S. Bolden
Dr. Willie Creagh Bolden
Nishia L. Brack
Susie Branch
Loviece Brazley
Gracie Briggs
Erica Dawn Brown
Jeanette B. Brown

Michele Brown
Olivia Brown
Barbara Buck
Nuntiata Buck
Dr. Januela Burt
Alice Butler
Juanita P. Chapman
Anna Chin
Leroy Chin
Priscilla Coatney
Luevenia Combest
Beverly Crandall
Lolita Cusic
Margaret Dugan

Juanita Eaton
Mary Edwards
Vyllorya A. Evans
Joyce Felder
Ruth Ferguson
Dora Finley
Norma Foster
Joyce Fourth
Zoë M. Isaac Gadsen
Shirley Green
Lucy Hall
Hazel Hammond
Willie Mae Harris
Dr. Dorothy I. Height

Sharon Harriston Henery

Doris Askew Hicks

Vivian Hinds

Margie M. Holmes

Wendy Johnson

Betty Jones

Doretha Manuel

Shirley McAlpin

Tonya McNeal

Dorothy McNeil

Rev. Clarence Miller

Flora Moore

Beverly Mullens

Ethel Peterson

Mrs. Luberta W. Portis

Nicale D. Portis

Carol Preston

La Ruth Pryor

Bessie Samples

Mrs. Edwena L. Seals

Melanie Shelwood

Renee Simmons

Mirtie Smith

Rosa Smith

Rita Stebbins

Betty Kleckley Stratford

Virginia Strong

Brenda R. Swanson

Louise E. Taylor

Sandra E. Thomas

Philonese Thompson

Julia Hardeman-Tsadick

Daisy A. Voigt

Lois Ward

Diana R. Weekes

Maddie West

Katherine L. Winslow

THE BOOKS

Anyone Can Bake
Royal Baking Powder Company
New York 1927

**The Black Family Dinner
Quilt Cookbook**
The Wimmer Companies
Memphis, TN 1993

Edith Barber's Cookbook
G. P. Putnam's Sons
New York 1940

**Family and Friends
Favorite Recipes**
Toulminville-Warren UMC
Mobile, AL 1998

Inglenook Cookbook
Brethren Publishing House
Elgin, IL 1911

Rumford Complete Cookbook
Tolman-University Press
Cambridge, MA 1931

***The Southern Cookbook of Fine
Old Recipes***
Culinary Arts Press
Reading, PA 1939

Tante Marie's French Kitchen
Oxford University Press
New York, 1949

The Twyner Family Cookbook

INDEX